THE NOT TO BE FORGOTTEN FORTIES

By Don Gwaltney

An eclectic recollection of important events and significant memorabilia for the reader who remembers — or wonders — what the world was like in the 1940s

Apple Core Press, Northbrook, IL

Books by Don Gwaltney

The Steak Lover's Handbook
Characters, Legends and $3 Bills
The Bandit Joaquin, An Orphaned Mexican's Search for Revenge in the California Gold Rush
The Not to be Forgotten Forties

First printing 1996

Library of Congress Cataloging-in-Publication Data:
Gwaltney, Don
    The Not to be Forgotten Forties – an eclectic recollection of important events and significant memorabilia for the reader who remembers – or wonders – what the world was like in the 1940s / by Don Gwaltney
p. cm.

Library of Congress Catalog Card Number: 96-97089
International Standard Book Number: 0-9639591-2-3

Design, Typography and Production by Connie and Stuart Cook and Katie Sekera
of GL Graphic Link, Inc. Lake Bluff, Illinois

Proofed and edited by Ann Johnson

Printed in the United States of America

 APPLE CORE PRESS
3453 West Commercial Avenue
Northbrook, Il 60062

ATTENTION CORPORATIONS, UNIVERSITIES, COLLEGES AND PROFESSIONAL ORGANIZATIONS: Quantity discounts are available on bulk purchases of this book for educational (or training) purposes (or fund raising). Special books or book excerpts can also be created to fit specific needs. For information, please contact the Fulfillment & Distribution Department at Apple Core Press (address above). Or, call 847-559-1374.

This book is dedicated
to my sidekick of 40 years
and chief researcher,
Carol June.

INNOCENCE ABROAD

What this book's about

This book is about people and events from the most mercurial decade in world history–the 1940s, a decade that began with the nation still mired in the throes of the Great Depression and ended with unparalleled prosperity. In the interim were The War and The Bomb.

When the forties began, we were never poorer. Ten years later, we were never more affluent.

It's about how life was 50 years ago. It was simple, but it was also changing. For entertainment, we "watched" the radio. The War put TV on hold. Saturday nights were special. We went out, usually to the movies. And censorship still existed.

Baseball was America's pastime then, too, and not even Hitler could shut it down. Strikes were not even considered.

For the first seven years of that decade, Joe Louis was the only black American on any center stage in America. By 1947, Jackie Robinson was playing major league baseball. And America was on its way, finally, to growing up.

In the beginning of that decade, jobs were hard to come by. And when they were available, men got them. Then the man of the house went off to war and the woman of the house went to work. And she has never looked back.

Back then, we knew who our neighbors were. Heck, we even visited them.

In the middle of the decade, the Dow Jones high hit 152 and unemployment was at 1.2%. A ticket to a Broadway show was $3 and a new girdle was three times that–$9. We only got paid two or three bucks an hour, but simple things like candy were five cents a bar and a loaf of bread was nine. For $1.28, you could buy enough ice cream for a good-sized birthday party, and you could buy bread, bacon and eggs for the whole family for less than a dollar.

And it is truly amazing how many things there are that you take for granted today that were not available only 50 years ago. Besides television and the computer, things like penicillin, polio shots, frozen foods, disposable diapers, Xerox, contact lenses, Frisbees, radar, credit cards, split atoms and THE PILL.

It was a time when it was fashionable to smoke cigarettes. Grass, we mowed. Coke was a soft drink and Pot was something you cooked soup in. Rock Music was something Grandma listened to and Aids were the folks who helped out at school, for no pay.

And we got married so we could live together. And thought we needed a husband to have a baby.

In the total course of earth events, on a chart of all the years of the lifetime of the planet since creation, the decade of the 1940's does not appear as just another tiny blip. It was indeed the most memorable decade in world history.

Enjoy the book. Have a great day.

Don Gwaltney

CONTENTS

The New York Times
June 11, 1940

The New York Times.

"All the News That's Fit to Print."

LATE CITY EDITION
Partly cloudy, warmer today, followed by showers tonight. Tomorrow fair, temperature unchanged.
Temperature Yesterday—Max., 78; Min., 65

Copyright, 1940, by The New York Times Company.

VOL. LXXXIX...No. 30,093.   Entered as Second-Class Matter, Postoffice, New York, N. Y.   NEW YORK, SATURDAY, JUNE, 15, 1940.   THREE CENTS NEW YORK CITY and Vicinity | FOUR CENTS Elsewhere Except In 7th and 8th Postal Zones

GERMANS OCCUPY PARIS, PRESS ON SOUTH; CAPTURE HAVRE, ASSAULT MAGINOT LINE; FRENCH ARMY INTACT; SPAIN SEIZES TANGIER

HITLER IS DOUBTED

Roosevelt Skeptical of Pledge He Will Not Cross Atlantic

HAS RECOLLECTIONS

U. S. Doing All It Can for Allies, He Asserts of French Appeal

By FELIX BELAIR Jr.

The International Situation

On the Battle Fronts

MOROCCANS MOVE IN

Spanish Troops Take Over Zone in Which U. S. Has Rights

'GIBRALTAR' NOW CRY

Madrid Students Parade and Shout for Return of the Famous Rock

By T. J. HAMILTON

FRENCH NOTE LULL

Battle Continues Along Front—At Some Points Its Violence Abates

ATTACK IS REPULSED

Nazi Losses Are Heavy in Maginot Assault— Loire Next Barrier

By H. ARCHAMBAULT

Will Fight On, British Insist, Even if the French Capitulate

London Letting Ally Make Decision on the Immediate Course as Help Is Speeded— New Nazi Peace Offensive Expected

2 FORCES TAKE CITY

Berlin Says Industrial Losses May Be Worst Feature for French

MONTMEDY CAPTURED

Anchor of Maginot Line Lost—Nazis Report Foe Is Routed

By C. BROOKS PETERS

COLONNA PROTESTS ON ITALIAN CHARGES

Envoy Sees Hull—Inquiry Here Widened—German Agent to U. S. Warns of Reprisals

ITALIANS IN CLASH ON FRENCH BORDER

Report Attack Repulsed— Fleet Action Revealed— Coast Is Shelled

By HERBERT L. MATTHEWS

TOURS ABANDONED AS FRENCH CAPITAL

Government Is Expected to Make Seat at Bordeaux— U. S. Move Is Awaited

By P. J. PHILIP

REICH TANKS CLANK IN CHAMPS-ELYSEES

Berlin Recounts Parade Into Paris—Third of Citizens Reported Remaining

British Call on U. S. for Munitions at Once; French Order 120 Bombers Here for 1941

By RAYMOND DANIELL

When World War I ended, the causes of World War II began. The League of Nations was The First World War's instrument of peace, but it left out the most powerful countries. It excluded Germany and the Soviet Union. And the United States never joined it. Throughout the thirties, while the world was in a great economic depression, extremist politics ruled the war-makers. Conquest was the only means of supporting the mighty armies, navies and air forces of Germany and Japan.

In July of 1937, Japan invaded China and the United States watched. In 1939, Germany invaded Poland and again the United States watched. But by the time the forties rolled around, world war was inevitable and with it the slaughter of millions of the world's peoples and much of its resources. For the first time, the use of highly destructive armament was at the disposal of all the world's powers and would be used literally across the globe. World War II lasted six years and one day and caused colossal loss. And when it was over, it removed from civilization several thousand maniacs but solved few of the world's problems.

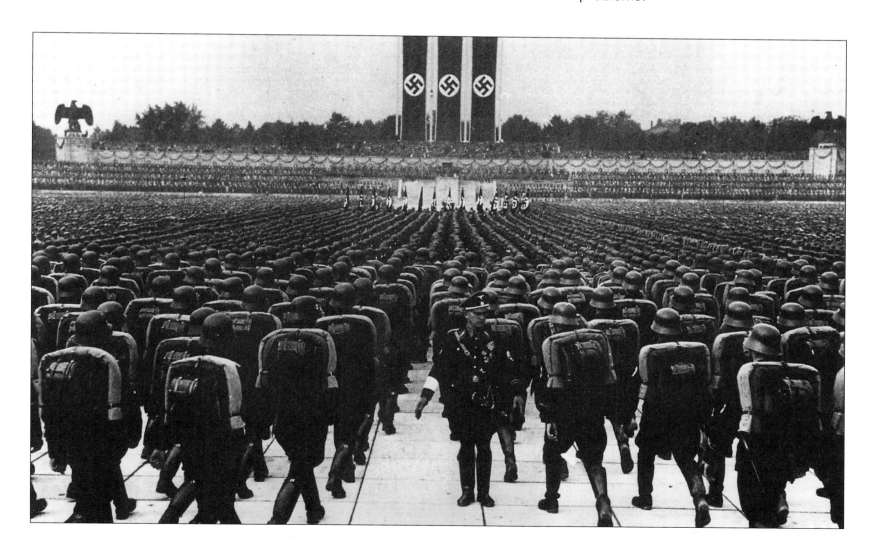

"I have said this before, but I shall say it again and again and again: Your boys are not going to be sent to any foreign wars."

Franklin Delano Roosevelt, October 30, 1940

3

The New York Times.

"All the News That's Fit to Print."

LATE CITY EDITION
POSTSCRIPT
Fair, not much change in temperature today. Tomorrow cloudy.
Temperature Yesterday—Max 66°-47°...

VOL. LXXXIX...No. 30,087.

NEW YORK, FRIDAY, MAY 10, 1940.

THREE CENTS NEW YORK CITY and Vicinity | FOUR CENTS Elsewhere Except in 7th and 8th Postal Zones

NAZIS INVADE HOLLAND, BELGIUM, LUXEMBOURG BY LAND AND AIR; DIKES OPENED; ALLIES RUSH AID

U.S. FREEZES CREDIT

President Acts to Guard Funds Here of Three Invaded Nations

SHIP RULING TODAY

Envoy Reports to Hull on Germany's Attacks by Air and Land

The International Situation

ALLIED HELP SPED

Netherland and Belgian Appeals Answered by British and French

TACTICS ARE WATCHED

London Thinks Move an Effort to Get Bases to Attack Britain

Italians Reported Massing

Bombs Drop on Swiss Soil

BRUSSELS IS RAIDED

400 Reported Killed— Troops Cross Border at Four Points

PARACHUTE INVASION

Mobilization Is Ordered and Allied Aid Asked— Luxembourg Attacked

AIR FIELDS BOMBED

Nazi Parachute Troops Land at Key Centers as Flooding Starts

RIVER MAAS CROSSED

Defenders Battle Foe in Sky, Claim 6 Planes as War Is Proclaimed

First Bombing in France

NAZIS SWOOP ON THE LOW COUNTRIES

By land and air German troops descended this morning upon the Netherlands, Belgium and Luxembourg. The principal land incursion into the Netherlands was at Roermond.

Ribbentrop Charges Allies Plotted With the Lowlands

By GEORGE AXELSSON

HOLLAND'S QUEEN PROTESTS INVASION

Wilhelmina Vows She and the Government Will Do Duty— Bars Negotiation With Foe

MUSSOLINI TO LET 'ONLY FACTS' SPEAK

Press Assures Yugoslavia, but Reminds Her of Fate of Poland and Norway

By HERBERT L. MATTHEWS

ICELAND OCCUPIED BY BRITISH FORCE

Secret Expedition Is Justified as Thwarting Action There by Germany

By JAMES MacDONALD

Chamberlain Saved by Nazi Blow In Low Countries, London Thinks

By RAYMOND DANIELL

Dispatches from Europe and the Far East are subject to censorship at the source.

Continued on Page Two
Continued on Page Seven
Continued on Page Three
Continued on Page Four
Continued on Page Five
Continued on Page Three

The New York Times
June 22, 1941

The New York Times front page, LATE CITY EDITION, Section 1. VOL. XC. No. 30,465. NEW YORK, SUNDAY, JUNE 22, 1941. TEN CENTS.

HITLER BEGINS WAR ON RUSSIA, WITH ARMIES ON MARCH FROM ARCTIC TO THE BLACK SEA; DAMASCUS FALLS; U. S. OUSTS ROME CONSULS

Why Adolph Hitler was ready for war and Uncle Sam wasn't

When the first World War ended, Germany was in a shambles. Hey, they lost! The Germans were shackled by the provisions of the Versailles Treaty, burdened by the necessity to pay reparations and controlled by the transfer of border regions to France and Poland. They were also hampered by inflation, class tension and confusion. But it took them but 10 short years to pull themselves up by their bootstraps and renew their ambitious quest to realize the potential to be the greatest of all the European powers.

The instrument of this amazing revival was an extremely unusual political party: the National Socialists, headed by its maniacal founder and leader, Adolph Hitler. The party had a bizarre mission - to purify the populace by totally eliminating what it considered undesirable factions. All Jews, gypsies and what other allegedly non-Teutonic elements stood in the wake would be exterminated. Deutschtum, an ideology of force and hatred, would scorn all ideas of compromise and smash all peoples and nations that stood in its way. In a few years, incredibly, this movement became immensely popular and by the late thirties was virtually unchallenged. How that could happen is the subject of dozens of other books already written. This one provides but a brief accounting of the fact that it did and of how powerful the movement became.

Hitler's political culture was hellbent on war and conquest. By 1938, the distortion was so great that a full 52 percent of Germany's governmental expenditures and 17 percent of its gross national product were funneled directly to manufacturing armaments. In 1938, Germany was spending more on building weapons than Britain, France and the United States combined.

In 1933, Germany's army was legally set at 100,000 men. By 1938, the German army consisted of 71 divisions. Within a year, 32 more were added, to bring the Nazi field army count to nearly three million men. The Luftwaffe grew even faster. In 1932, only 36 aircraft were built. By 1938, there were 4,000 new planes, enough to equip 302 squadrons. And the German navy had increased by fivefold and was spending 12 times more than before Hitler became dictator. In 1938, the European balance of power once again weighed in Germany's favor.

All this rearmament was unbelievably expensive, but the tactics of Hitler's ideology allowed for payment. To get five more divisions of troops, iron ore and oil fields, a world-class metal industry and some $200 million in gold and foreign-exchange reserves, Hitler acquired Austria. To get more ores and metals plus more aircraft, tanks and weapons, Hitler acquired Czechoslovakia. This allowed Hitler to maintain his current rearmament program and gave him the answer for further growth: continued acquisition. His Nazi regime would subsist on conquest. No country on earth would be spared in his quest. Only by constant conquering could he achieve his dream of complete purification and, with it, Jewish annihilation.

Maniacal, yes. It was an insane dream backed by fanatical obsession. And there was little the rest of the world would do but await the consequences, which would be horrible. There was no chance for a German victory. America was still strong; in 1938, it manufactured a whopping 28.7% of the world's goods, compared to an output of but 13.2% for Germany. And Russia was in second place, with 17.6%.

In America, Franklin Roosevelt had different problems: He was trying to put an end to an economic depression. A war would stimulate that economy.

Nevertheless, Hitler was getting ready for war. Dumb, blind rage ruled the day.

On December 7, 1941, *sailors at the Ford Island Naval Air Station in Hawaii were stunned by the explosion of the battleship Arizona. The Japanese air raid on the Pearl Harbor anchorage abruptly wiped out America's battleship force.*

Why the Japanese caught Uncle Sam sleeping at Pearl Harbor on December 7, 1941

It was not just because the American fleet decided to sleep in on that fateful Sunday morning. It traces back 20 years, to the 1921 - 1922 Washington Conference, when America elected to retreat into at least relative diplomatic isolationism, for reasons best explained in a far more complete treatise of world history than what is to be found in the pages of this book. However, for speedy learning or reminding, here it is in one brief chapter.

In 1921, the Big Three in world-power politics were Germany, Russia and the United States, despite the fact that the first-named had just been decisively whipped, the second had collapsed in revolution and the third, although clearly the world's most popular nation, had preferred to retreat from the center of world diplomacy. Italy was in the process of allowing Benito Mussolini to turn it into a Fascist state and was relatively quiescent. Japan, too, was tranquil for the moment. France and England, badly wounded from the rigors of World War I, were in the process of girding up for a future German resurgence. Clues of that came quickly; as early as 1923, Germany defaulted on reparation payments.

Except for the wild rise and fall of the American Stock Market, most of the world was rather subdued through most of the 1920's. The world had diminished and needed time to recover. Around eight million men were killed on World War I battlefields, with another seven million permanently disabled and a further 15 million seriously wounded. In addition, there were millions of civilian casualties. There were also millions of "birth deficits," caused by so many men off to war and thus not able to increase populations. The final casualty count has been estimated as high as a whopping total of 60-million people.

The material costs of the First World War were also shocking, so huge they were virtually incomprehensible. One calculation set it at $260 billion, equal to six and a half times the sum of all the national debt accumulated in the world from the end of the 18th century to the beginning of World War I.

Outright withdrawal was America's basic reaction to the horrors of that war. And so, while Mussolini whipped Italy into a state of force and conquest and Hitler did likewise in Germany, America merely slept and ignored what was happening in the rest of the world. By 1938, world production was again booming, more than double what it was in 1921. Germany had by then more than doubled its manufacturing production, as had Russia, Italy, England and France. And the sleeper among the world powers: Japan, which was suddenly manufacturing at a rate five and a half times greater than at the beginning of World War I. America was the only powerful nation to not double its output in that period. America was not even up 50%.

Japan's remarkable surge exposed alarming warning signs to the rest of the world. Japan did not have the natural resources to match its suddenly voracious appetite. Its factories depended more and more on imported raw materials. And its government expenditures were not headed to domestic enhancement but to its military. By 1938, Japan's armed services were taking 70% of government expenditure. The Imperial Japanese Navy, legally restricted by the Washington Treaty to slightly over half the size of either the British or American navy, was in reality far more powerful.

Japan's growth had shot far beyond treaty limits. While 8,000 tons was the number set by the treaty for heavy cruiser displacement, Japan's cruisers weighed in at 14,000 tons. Japan's major warships were heavily armed and fast, its battleships were newly modernized and its newest ships were the largest in the world. But, fearsome as the Japanese navy was, it was in the skies where they really ruled. By the late 1930s, the Japanese could boast 3,000 aircraft and 3,500 highly-trained pilots. This awesome air army was based mainly on the 10 aircraft carriers in the Japanese fleet, but also included land-based bomber and torpedo planes. And Japanese torpedoes were the world's most powerful.

The Japanese army was also expanding at an alarming rate. In the four years prior to 1941, the number of division and air squadrons more than doubled. In 1941, Japan had 51 active service divisions, 133 air squadrons, 10 depot divisions for training and independent brigade and garrison troops equal to another 30 divisions. By the time the Japanese hit Pearl Harbor, the army consisted of over one million men, backed by two million trained reserves. And the army's own aircraft had an additional 2,000 planes to add to Japan air might. At the start of the war, the Japanese had already built 1,000 of the formidable Zeroes, the best fighter planes in the world at that time.

The cost of sheer maintenance of this military force was astronomical, compounded by the fact that it was actively employed in war against the Chinese. The "China Incident" of the late thirties, as Tokyo referred to it, was costing Japan $5 million a day. It was also creating a rapidly increasing national debt and a dramatic shrinkage of raw materials. To continue on its current growth pattern, Japan would have to expand by conquering other lands. To the north, an attempted conquest of Russia was certainly considered. But, by then the Japanese had to admit Red Army superiority, both in the air and certainly on land, where Russian tanks were much larger and far more numerous. A war across massive stretches of land would

The New York Times
December 8, 1941

surely result in Russian victory. Japan's strength lay on the open seas and in the jungles of the islands of those seas.

It should have been no secret, especially to the isolationists in Washington, that America would become Japan's prime target. To ensure economic security, Japan would have to attack the sleeping giant. Japan was on a journey of no return, even if it meant attacking a country with twice the population, 17 times the national income, with the ability to produce five times as much steel, seven times as much coal and an overall industrial potential easily 10 times greater.

By 1941, the Japanese military had put Japan into an economic hole with no escape. Not to attack would mean financial ruin. Despite overwhelming odds against, the Japanese military leaders made the fateful decision to plunge forward. It was a decision born of patriotic fanaticism and no logic, bordering on the incredible and the absurd. In the history of the world, it is impossible to recount a dumber call by military strategists.

In late November, 1941, Japan went to sea. Destination: Pearl Harbor.

9

ALMOST THE LAST NEUTRAL

The New York Times
December 9, 1941

The New York Times.

"All the News That's Fit to Print."

LATE CITY EDITION
Cloudy followed by clearing and colder today. Tomorrow fair and moderately cold.
Temperature Yesterday—Max. 64; Min. 35

VOL. XCI. No. 30,638.

NEW YORK, TUESDAY, DECEMBER 9, 1941.

THREE CENTS NEW YORK CITY and Vicinity

U.S. DECLARES WAR, PACIFIC BATTLE WIDENS; MANILA AREA BOMBED; 1,500 DEAD IN HAWAII; HOSTILE PLANES SIGHTED AT SAN FRANCISCO

TURN BACK TO SEA

Two Formations Neared City on Radio Beams, Then Went Astray

ALARM IS WIDESPREAD

Whole Coast Has a Nervous Night—Many Cities Blacked Out

By LAWRENCE E. DAVIES
Special to The New York Times.

SAN FRANCISCO, Dec. 8—Two formations of "many planes," described as undoubtedly enemy aircraft, flew over the San Francisco Bay area tonight, it was announced officially by Brig. Gen. William O. Ryan, commander of the Fourth Interceptor Command, after a progressive blackout had blotted out naval and military establishments and whole cities along the Pacific Coast.

Conflicting reports spread, contributing to the "war of nerves," as the sirens wailed and broadcasting were silenced.

After another spokesman, through an error, had declared the blackout to be an air raid test, General Ryan said at the Presidio that it was no test but "the real thing."

The ships were detected first about 100 miles at sea, he said. In two formations they headed for the Monterey Peninsula, about eighty miles south of this city, and for San Francisco itself.

Philippines Pounded All Day As Raiders Strike at Troops

Air Base Near Capital Among Targets Hit by Japanese—Landing on Lubang With Aid of Fifth Columnists Reported

By H. FORD WILKINS
Wireless to The New York Times.

MANILA, Tuesday, Dec. 9—After a day of widespread aerial attacks throughout the Philippines, Japanese bombers swept in over Manila Bay early this morning and attacked Nichols Field, the United States Army air base on the outskirts of this capital, and simultaneously reports were received of a Japanese landing on Lubang Island, off the northwestern tip of Mindoro.

This morning's attack, which began shortly after 3 o'clock, was the first in the Manila area. The damage was believed to have been slight, but some casualties were reported. [A National Broadcasting Company correspondent reported that an official statement issued in Manila after the raid said: "In the raid on Nichols Field, which was conducted by approximately ten Japanese bombers, one hangar was damaged and one officers' quarters was burned. The casualty list consists of one soldier killed and twelve wounded—all Americans."]

The reported landing on Lubang, sixty miles southwest of Manila, was not officially confirmed, but the reports received credence here. [Other unconfirmed reports, relayed by the Columbia Broadcasting System, told of landings in the Davao region, on the southern island of Mindanao.]

The Manila area's first experience with bombs was a climax to a day and night of tension and activity. The explosions could be

PLANES GUARD CITY FROM AIR ATTACKS

Army Interceptors Join the Navy Patrols—Anti-Aircraft Apparatus Set Up Here

While long lines of men of fighting age waited impatiently outside of every Army, Navy and

MALAYA THWARTS PUSH BY JAPANESE

Thailand Capitulates and Is Seen Virtually in Axis—Two Raids on Singapore

By F. TILLMAN DURDIN
Wireless to The New York Times.

SINGAPORE, Dec. 8—The Japa-

1 BATTLESHIP LOST

Capsized in Pearl Harbor, Destroyer Is Blown Up, Other Ships Hurt

FLEET NOW IS FIGHTING

Aid Rushed to Hawaii— Some Congressmen Sharply Critical

By CHARLES HURD
Special to The New York Times.

WASHINGTON, Dec. 8—The Battle of the Pacific opened tonight over a 5,000-mile "front" from Hawaii to the Philippines while a badly battered United States Fleet fought back at Japanese sea and air forces that launched severe attacks yesterday afternoon.

Tonight the Japanese were reported to be launching their main attack at the Philippines, particularly at Palawan, the greatest natural harbor in the archipelago. That attack was preceded today, according to reports from Manila, by an onslaught against the United States military air fields there, which put these out of commission for the time being and set fire to storage tanks containing vital gasoline for air operations.

The Japanese Sunday attack on Hawaii was reported in informed quarters to have been launched from the mandated islands, rather than from Japan proper, and aircraft carriers presumably approached

The President signs the declaration of war. *Associated Press Wirephoto*

LARGE U.S. LOSSES CLAIMED BY JAPAN

Tokyo Lists 2 Battleships

UNITY IN CONGRESS

Only One Negative Vote as President Calls to War and Victory

ROUNDS OF CHEERS

Miss Rankin's Is Sole 'No' as Both Houses Act in Quick Time

By FRANK L. KLUCKHOHN
Special to The New York Times.

WASHINGTON, Dec. 8—The United States today formally declared war on Japan. Congress, with only one dissenting vote, approved the resolution in the record time of 33 minutes after President Roosevelt denounced Japanese aggression in ringing tones. His personally delivered his message to a joint session of the Senate and House. At 4:10 P. M. he affixed his signature to the resolution.

There was no debate like that between April 2, 1917, when President Wilson requested war against Germany, and April 6, when a declaration of war was approved by Congress.

President Roosevelt spoke only 6 minutes and 30 seconds today as compared with Woodrow Wilson's 29 minutes and 34 seconds.

The vote today against Japan was 82 to 0 in the Senate and 388 to 1 in the House. The lone vote against the resolution in the House was that of Miss Jeanette Rankin, Republican, of Montana. "No" was greeted with boos

The President's Message

Following is the text of President Roosevelt's war message to Congress, as recorded by THE NEW YORK TIMES from a broadcast:

Mr. Vice President, Mr. Speaker, members of the Senate and the House of Representatives:

"We are now in this war. We are all in it all the way. Every single man, woman and child is a partner in the most tremendous undertaking of our American history. We must share together the bad news and the good news, the defeats and the victories — the changing fortunes of war."

— Franklin Delano Roosevelt, Address to the Nation, December 9, 1941

The New York Times
December 12, 1941

"All the News That's Fit to Print"

The New York Times.

Copyright, 1941, by The New York Times Company.

LATE CITY EDITION
Fair, slowly rising temperature today. Tomorrow cloudy, moderately cold, occasional snow.
Temperature Yesterday—Max. 34; Min. 24

VOL. XCI. No. 30,688.

Entered as Second-Class Matter, Postoffice, New York, N. Y.

NEW YORK, FRIDAY, DECEMBER 12, 1941.

THREE CENTS NEW YORK CITY and Vicinity

U.S. NOW AT WAR WITH GERMANY AND ITALY; JAPANESE CHECKED IN ALL LAND FIGHTING; 3 OF THEIR SHIPS SUNK, 2D BATTLESHIP HIT

BLOCKED IN LUZON

But Japanese Put Small Force Ashore in South of Philippine Island

SABOTEURS ARE HELD

Some in Manila Seized for Spreading Rumor About City Water

By H. FORD WILKINS
Wireless to THE NEW YORK TIMES

MANILA, Friday, Dec. 12—The United States Army Far East headquarters announced today that a small Japanese invasion force was reported to have pushed ashore at Legaspi, Southern Luzon, and "the enemy has improved his strength in Northern Luzon," where, however, the situation remains unchanged yesterday. The announcement added that the report of the Legaspi landing was still unconfirmed and there were no details.

[Small forces of Japanese apparently have been landed at Legaspi, it was said officially three hours after the morning communiqué had said merely that the Legaspi development had not yet been confirmed, a United Press dispatch from Manila said.]

There was no further indication of the progress of the sea war. The office of Admiral Thomas C. Hart, commander in chief of the United States Asiatic Fleet, remained silent.

One Japanese plane was shot down by an American fighter near Bancayan, in the mountain mining district.

2,000 Families Are Moved

Manila took further emergency measures to evacuate portions of the old walled city. The Red Cross supervised the removal of 2,000 families, loading them into buses and trucks and taking them to safety zones considerably removed from the city. Identification cards were issued and checked as the evacuees lined up for removal.

With Lieut. Gen. Douglas MacArthur's United States Far Eastern forces fully in control of the North Luzon invasion threat and his air force sufficiently active to disperse Japanese raiders headed for Manila, his intelligence service turned yesterday to mopping up fifth columnists.

Their latest trick was to circulate rumors that the city water supply had been poisoned. Army, city and government officials quickly scotched the rumors with assurances and proof that nothing whatever was wrong with the water supply. Several persons were arrested, including air-raid wardens, on a city-wide house-to-house campaign warning the people against "impure water."

Several persons entered hospitals asserting that they had been poisoned, but examination disclosed that nothing was wrong with them but upset stomachs and fear. Elaborate analysis proved that the water they drank was not contaminated.

The official communiqué asserting that mopping-up operations were progressing heightened the morale of the nation, suddenly plunged into total war and the first taste of conflict in forty years.

The sinking of a United States Army transport in Manila Bay, as announced by Tokyo, was denied officially here yesterday.

Interned Japanese, numbering around 2,000, were revealed to be extremely uncomfortable under the threat of bombs from Japanese planes, recognizing that bombs do not distinguish nationalities.

Legaspi Move Discounted

MANILA, Friday, Dec. 12 (U.P)—The small Japanese landings at Legaspi, a port of about 38,000

Continued on Page Eight

Line-Up of World War II

THE ALLIES

Australia	Haiti
*Belgium	*Honduras
Canada	Netherlands Indies
China	New Zealand
Costa Rica	Nicaragua
Cuba	†Norway
†Czecho-Slovakia	*Panama
Dominican Republic	†Poland
*El Salvador	South Africa
Free France	†Soviet Union
Great Britain	United States
*Greece	†Yugoslavia
Guatemala	

THE AXIS

Finland	Japan
Germany	Manchukuo
Hungary	Rumania
Italy	Slovakia

*Have declared war on Japan only.
†At war only with Germany, Italy and their European allies.

CITY CALM AND GRIM AS THE WAR WIDENS

Loyalty and a Determination to Win Are Evident in Every Class and National Group

The people of New York City received the news that we are at war with Germany and Italy as well as Japan with profound calm and a quiet, stern determination to see it through, no matter how long it takes. Patriotism and loyalty were the spontaneous order of the day in every household, in every business office, every factory, every school and every institution. The whole city rallied in support of the war.

All over the city the Stars and Stripes flew proudly from public and private buildings, and those in charge of Army, Navy, Coast Guard and civilian defense organizations swung promptly and forcefully into action to protect the city

Continued on Page Twenty-one

The International Situation

FRIDAY, DECEMBER 12, 1941

The United States declared war yesterday on Germany and Italy. Congress acted swiftly without a dissenting vote. [Page 1, Column 8.] Then, without debate, it passed a bill to permit the use of all United States land forces anywhere in the world. [Page 1, Column 7.]

This action coincided with good news from the Pacific. Washington announced the sinking of a Japanese battleship, a cruiser and a destroyer and reported severe damage to a second battleship by bomb hits. [Page 1, Column 3, Map, Page 8.]

The American declaration came within a few hours after Germany and Italy had declared war on the United States. The Reich's declaration was made in a diplomatic note and in a Reichstag address by Adolf Hitler. [Page 4, Column 1.] Benito Mussolini proclaimed Italy's declaration. [Page 4, Column 5.]

In London, where news of America's full entry into the world war brought predictions of an Allied grand strategy [Page 12, Column 5], Prime Minister Churchill declared that the Allies would win ultimately at any cost. [Page 1, Column 4.] Mexico broke off relations with Germany and Italy, while ten other Latin-American nations declared war on those countries or prepared to take that step. [Page 9, Column 1.]

The Soviet radio asserted that any Axis hopes for a separate peace with Russia were in vain. The radio declared that Russia was determined to fight alongside the United States and Britain until the Allies won. [Page 19, Column 3.]

In all of yesterday's land fighting, Japan was checked. In the Philippines, attempts by win a firm foothold on Luzon appeared smashed, except for a landing of parachutists at an airport 140

U. S. FLIERS SCORE

Bombs Send Battleship, Cruiser and Destroyer to the Bottom

MARINES KEEP WAKE

Small Force Fights Off Foe Despite Loss of Some of Planes

By CHARLES HURD
Special to THE NEW YORK TIMES

WASHINGTON, Dec. 11—A Japanese battleship, a cruiser and a destroyer have been sunk in the Pacific and a second battleship badly damaged by bomb hits, the United States forces announced in communiqués today recounting their first major victories in the warfare that began last Sunday with surprise Japanese attacks.

Damage to the second battleship was revealed tonight in a Navy communiqué, which said a man-of-war of the Kongo class had been hit by Navy patrol planes off the coast of Luzon. This was "the second battleship to be bombed effectively by United States forces," the communiqué asserted.

The battleship sunk, also of the Kongo class, was believed to have been the 29,330-ton Haruna. She went down after having been set afire by aerial bombardment north of Luzon. She had been supporting an attack in which the Japanese effected a landing at Appari, a remote village on the northern Philippine coast, separated from Manila by mountains and forests. The cruiser, unidentified except that it was of the light class, and the destroyer were sunk also by fliers who took off from Wake

Continued on Page Six

Left: The President set his signature to the act against Germany. Center: He checked the time with Senator Tom Connally. Right: After that he placed the United States officially at war with Italy.

Associated Press Wirephotos

AXIS TO GET LESSON, CHURCHILL WARNS

He Announces Replacement of Libyan General—Upholds Phillips's Judgment

By CABLE TO THE NEW YORK TIMES

LONDON, Dec. 11—Prime Minister Winston Churchill delivered a review of the war in the Pacific, North Africa, Russia and the Atlantic today that contained a compound of gloom and of optimism, but he ended with this ringing declaration:

"Just handfuls and cliques of wicked men and their military or party organizations have been able to bring these hideous evils upon mankind. It would indeed bring shame upon our generation if we did not teach them a lesson which will not be forgotten in a thousand years."

Precedes Declarations

He spoke to the House of Commons before the Axis war declarations and the United States' reply.

Mr. Churchill gave hitherto unpublished details about the sinking of the Prince of Wales and the Repulse, which made plain that the British had lost the use of airdromes on the Malay Peninsula and that the ships had had to rely solely on their anti-aircraft guns for protection against the attacking planes. In so doing he stoutly defended the judgment whereby Vice Admiral Sir Tom S. V. Phillips, who appeared tonight to have been lost, undertook an attack on Japanese transports that resulted in the sinkings of the warships.

Mr. Churchill announced that Lieut. Gen. Sir Alan Gordon Cunningham had been replaced in Libya by Major Gen. Neil Methuen Ritchie, adding that General Cunningham "has been reported by medical authorities to be suffering from serious overstrain and was granted sick leave."

General Ritchie, the new commander of the Eighth Army, is 44 years old. His was one of three "young-men" appointments to the General Staff that were made last June. In the last war he was commissioned a second lieutenant in the Black Watch at the age of seventeen and was a captain when he was twenty. He fought in France, Mesopotamia and Palestine and received the Distinguished Service Order and the Military Cross.

Mr. Churchill gave an indication of the size of British and Allied losses in mercantilemen in the Battle of the Atlantic for November that would, from the statement, appear to have been no greater than 100,000 tons. This would be a

Continued on Page Three

Our Declaration of War

Special to THE NEW YORK TIMES

WASHINGTON, Dec. 11—Following are the texts of the documents wherein the President asked a war declaration against Germany and Italy, and Congress acted:

The President's Message

To the Congress of the United States:

On the morning of Dec. 11 the Government of Germany, pursuing its course of world conquest, declared war against the United States.

The long-known and the long-expected has thus taken place. The forces endeavoring to enslave the entire world now are moving toward this hemisphere.

Never before has there been a greater challenge to life, liberty and civilization.

Delay invites great danger. Rapid and united effort by all of the peoples of the world who are determined to remain free will insure a world victory of the forces of justice and of righteousness over the forces of savagery and of barbarism.

Italy also has declared war against the United States.

I therefore request the Congress to recognize a state of war between the United States and Germany, and between the United States and Italy.

FRANKLIN D. ROOSEVELT.

The War Resolution

Declaring that a state of war exists between the Government of Germany and the government and the people of the United States and making provision to prosecute the same.

Whereas the Government of Germany has formally declared war against the government and the people of the United States of America:

Therefore, be it

Resolved by the Senate and House of Representatives of the United States of America in Congress assembled, that the state of war between the United States and the Government of Germany which has thus been thrust upon the United States is hereby formally declared; and the President is hereby authorized and directed to employ the entire naval and military forces of the United States and the resources of the government to carry on war against the Government of Germany; and, to bring the conflict to a successful termination, all of the resources of the country are hereby pledged by the Congress of the United States.

(An identic resolution regarding Italy was adopted.)

Secretary Knox Visits Honolulu; Bases There Were Raided 5 Times

Special to THE NEW YORK TIMES

WASHINGTON, Dec. 11—The Navy Department announced tonight that Secretary Frank Knox had arrived in Honolulu this afternoon.

There was no previous announcement that he had left for Hawaii, nor was there any intimation of the specific purpose of his visit.

WASHINGTON, Dec. 11 (U.P)—Delegate Samuel W. King of Hawaii disclosed tonight after a telephone conversation with Governor Joseph B. Poindexter that twenty Japanese planes were shot down during the Sunday raid on Pearl Harbor.

Mr. King said the information was authorized for release in Hawaii by Lieut. Gen. Walter C. Short and that Mr. Poindexter was permitted to make the disclosure by transpacific radio-telephone.

Mr. Poindexter told Mr. King that "civilian morale is 100 per cent throughout the territory.

Continued on Page Seventeen

WAR OPENED ON US

Congress Acts Quickly as President Meets Hitler Challenge

A GRIM UNANIMITY

Message Warns Nation Foes Aim to Enslave This Hemisphere

By FRANK L. KLUCKHORN
Special to THE NEW YORK TIMES

WASHINGTON, Dec. 11—The United States declared war today on Germany and Italy's Axis partners. This nation acted swiftly after Germany formally declared war on us and Italy followed the German lead. Thus, President Roosevelt told Congress in his message, the long-known and the long-expected has taken place.

"The forces endeavoring to enslave the entire world now are moving toward this hemisphere," he said.

"Never before has there been a greater challenge to life, liberty and civilization."

Delay, the President said, invites great danger. But he added: "Rapid and united effort by all of the peoples of the world who are determined to remain free will insure a world victory of the forces of justice and righteousness over the forces of savagery and barbarism."

For the first time in its history the United States finds itself at war against powers in both the Atlantic and the Pacific.

Quick and Unanimous Answer

Congress acted not only rapidly but without a dissenting vote on the Axis challenge. Within two and three-quarters hours after war was started in the Senate and House at 12:26 P. M., the President had signed the declarations against Germany and Italy. Seventy-two hours previously the Japanese attack on Hawaii had brought about the declaration of war against the other Axis partner.

CONGRESS KILLS BAN ON AN A. E. F.

Swift Action Without Debate— Service Terms Are Extended to Six Months After War

Special to THE NEW YORK TIMES

WASHINGTON, Dec. 11—Congress swiftly eliminated prohibitions against American expeditionary forces today and continued terms of enlistment or induction to a date six months after hostilities end. Acting without debate, the two houses dropped the A. E. F. ban by removing restrictions in the Selective Service Act on the use of troops outside the Western Hemisphere.

A ranking member of the committee was unable to say tonight what the exact amount of the bill was, but he said he was "satisfied it is above $10,500,000,000." He added that the amendments "approve" by the committee were mostly for new items, regarded as emergency ones by the Army and the Navy and Coast Guard. If authorized, the measure would set a record for the size of a single appropriation bill.

Fund for Army Pay Specified

Among the amendments approved by the committee was one setting at $314,000,000 the supplemental item for pay of the Army, but immediately following it was a provision that this amount should not be taken to mean the limit of the Army inducted or enlisted thousands of new personnel. If this took place, under the amendment appropriated, actual authority would be granted for pay of the personnel under Congressional promise to pass deficiency bills to whatever extent was necessary.

HONOLULU, Dec. 11 (U.P)—In addition to the two deadly attacks on the United States naval base at Pearl Harbor last Sunday, Japanese bombers followed with a third attack later that day and with a fourth Monday morning, it is possible to disclose today for the first time.

Censorship permits a cautious description of the attack. A few seconds after the first bombers came over, with the rising sun insignia of Japan on their wings, defending anti-aircraft batteries sent up a heavy barrage.

Within a few minutes heavy clouds of black smoke began rolling up from Pearl Harbor, fourteen miles from Honolulu.

Planes roared in over the harbor, dropping bombs on navy centers and ships. Torpedo planes splashed

Continued on Page Eleven

"Civilian defense measures are working without a hitch," he added.

HONOLULU, Dec. 11 (U.P)—In addition to the two deadly attacks on the United States naval base...

Some $390,000,000 was added to the bill for military air construction. The Signal Corps also received a sizable increase for construction and equipment, while the Navy were granted increases of many millions for landing fields, yards and docks. The Coast Guard received $4,750,000 for extraordinary expenses and $8,743,000 for new equipment.

The Army Chief of Staff received $125,000,000 as an emergency fund, to be accounted for by Congress every three months, and various sums were voted for additions to forts and posts within the United States.

The measure changing the Selective Service Act regarding the tenure of service and the extent of service came on the heels of action by both houses in declaring war on Germany and Italy, following up a heavy barrage.

Grim Mood in Congress

Congress acted in a grim mood, but without excitement. Not only on the floors of the Senate and House, but in the galleries the grim mood prevailed. President Roosevelt, busy at the White House directing the battle and production effort as Commander in Chief, did not appear for what was an unusual test, as he did when war was declared upon Japan.

There was a deeply solemn undertone as the members assembled at noon. Senator Walsh, chairman of the Senate Naval Affairs Committee, had announced that the

Continued on Page Five

Nazis on the way to Stalingrad. *When the Germans first entered Russia, anti-communist feelings were high and the Russians considered the Nazis their liberators. These Ukrainian peasants showered them with flowers. But the Nazis did not take advantage of this feeling. They were brutal to Russian citizens and Russia then fought back.*

In February of 1943, relentless Soviet infantry attacks finally overwhelmed the last isolated pockets of German resistance and the Germans surrendered their entire Sixth Army. Only 90,000 Germans were taken prisoners. The Soviets later announced that they had removed 147,000 German and 47,000 Soviets from the city for burial. Horribly, history lost track of the rest of the Sixth Army. Later, only 60,000 German prisoners were still alive to be marched through the streets of Moscow. Only 5,000 of these prisoners ever returned to Germany, and many of these did not return home until 1955.

15

If Mad Adolph had gotten his way, Russians would have been obliterated.

September 29, 1941

TO: Army Group North

FR: Adolph Hitler

RE: Future of the City of Petersburg

I.   The Fuhrer is determined to remove the city of Petersburg from the face of the earth. After the defeat of Soviet Russia there can be no interest in the continued existence of this large urban area.

II. It is intended to encircle the town and level it to the ground by means of artillery bombardment using every calibre of weapon, and continual air bombardment.

III. Requests for surrender resulting from the city's encirclement will be denied, since the problem of relocating and feeding the population cannot and should not be solved by us. In this war for our very existence, there can be no interest on our part in maintaining even a part of this large urban population.

Adolph Hitler sounding off to peoples too encumbered to applaud.

Wouldn't you think that

somebody

from a nation full of

reasonably ethical

brewmeisters,

sausage stuffers,

steam fitters,

scientists

and Lutheran ministers

would have stepped forward

and grabbed this

diabolical maniac

and bashed him across his mustache

with a crowbar

and then dragged him

across Berlin

and thrown his

worthless bones

butt first

into a

fiery furnace?

Hermann Wilhelm
Goering

19

Hermann the aviator, accordionist, proud papa, collector, downhill skier, bow hunter, deer slayer, pal of Adolph, No. 2 Nazi, mass murderer

Hermann Wilhelm Goering was a self-indulgent pig whose bizarre indulgences benefited hugely from his 12 - year stint as Hitler's No. Two man. He was also a lousy Reichmarshal, and it remains a mystery (to me, anyway...maybe you know or can find out what Adolph had on him) why Hitler put up with him. He was notorious for making colossal military blunders and kept at it throughout the war.

To his credit, Goering did have a good start in his military career. Unlike pal Adolph, he did well in World War I. As a young fighter pilot in that war, he earned the distinction of ace and held Germany's prized Pour le Merite.

He then capitalized on those achievements by making conspicuous consumption a fine art. That started back in February of 1933, when Hitler made Goering head of the Prussian police, a job Hermann kept until Hitler gave him overall control of German war industry in January of 1940. In May of 1940, Hitler appointed Hermann the head of the German Luftwaffe, a post he somehow managed to hold onto throughout the duration of the war. By then, power had started going to his head and belly and he began acting as if he should not be bothered to even think about any duties connected with Luftwaffe commander in chief.

When Herman first got the lofty assignments, he was lean and, as you would expect, mean. He quickly grew into the assignments, literally. He quickly became a fat slob and made a very fat life for himself. That life was not centered around Nazi command posts but a hunting lodge that also served as an art gallery that he had built to his specifications in the Schorfheide, northeast of Berlin. It was a palace on vast game preserve grounds. Hermann's visions of grandeur had himself pictured as both architect and artist. He kept scores of real architects busy, not only at Schorfheide but also at several nearby castles, hunting lodges and estates. He also kept tailors busy designing costumes for the various roles he played. His wardrobe included more than 500 uniforms, plus numerous sporting and leisure outfits like the one pictured here.

One of the new titles he assigned himself was that of "Reichsjagermeister," which made him Head Ranger of the Reich. He had medieval huntsman uniforms designed for that, and wore them with great flamboyance. In his personal scrapbook, which you can view on microfilm at America's Library of Congress, you can see him in many of these costumes. He loved to toboggan, ski, shoot deer with guns and aim at targets with bow and arrow, show off his extensive medals collection, review troops, ride in great limousines, strut in front of his pretty daughter after spoiling her with outlandish gifts, guzzle booze and fill his days with all sorts of clownish activities.

As a military strategist, he was a total boob. He started the Battle of Britain by sending 70 Luftwaffe planes over to bomb docks in South Wales, promising pal Adolph that Berlin would be safe from retaliation. A month later, the RAF bombed Berlin. In that bombing raid, the air battle was fierce. The British lost 19 planes, while the defenders of "impregnable" Berlin lost 28.

A year later, Hermann screwed up again in a manner that would surely have gotten him fired in any other country. With German troops surrounded at Stalingrad, he persuaded Hitler to hold on because his Luftwaffe would be able to drop in with supplies. Mind you, some 700 tons of supplies would be needed daily, and for this 500 planes would be necessary as well as good weather and low losses. Hermann didn't know it, but only 300 planes were currently available and the Stalingrad airfields were in very poor condition. To amass the necessary air power, Hermann commandeered planes from the Battle of Britain, which he was already losing. The Stalingrad air-rescue attempt was made, and before the siege was over the Germans lost nearly 500 planes. It was a total disaster, both in the air and on the ground. The Soviets later claimed they removed 147,000 German soldiers from the city for burial and took 90,000 prisoners to Moscow. Of those, only 5,000 ever returned to Germany, the last as late as 1955.

Despite the screw-ups, Hitler kept Hermann on the job as Luftwaffe commander. And the excesses continued. In January of 1945, Germany was about at the end of its rope. This did not deter Hermann. His birthday was coming up, and Hermann's staff used up hundreds of litres of scarce petrol to bring Hermann birthday presents from Berlin to one of his palatial estates, Karinhall. It has been reported that the 150 birthday party guests consumed 100 bottles of fine, confiscated French champagne, 85 bottles of French cognac, 180 bottles of vintage wine, 50 bottles of imported liqueurs, 500 imported cigars and 4,000 Camels and Lucky Strikes.

A few short months later, when Hermann was recovered from his hangover, he fired off a message to Adolph. He offered to take over the leadership of the Reich if Hitler were unable to continue with that job while being besieged in Berlin. Hitler did not appreciate the offer. He ordered Hermann's arrest. That was on April 23, 1945.

The arrest was apparently botched, because it was Hermann who surrendered himself to the U.S. Seventh Army in East Prussia 16 days later, on May 9, 1945.

Hermann went on trial at Nuremberg the following November for his part in his country's war crimes. The charges against him were numerous, and he was sentenced to death. But this particular naughty Nazi remained unrepentant to the end. On the eve of his scheduled execution, he cheated the hangman by taking his final cocktail: It consisted of cyanide.

At the end of his life, Hitler did finally realize what a clown Hermann was. In a brief moment of sanity, just before committing suicide, Hitler turned to one of his aides and said, "Bauer, my tombstone should bear the words, 'He was the victim of his generals.' "

Hermann was not a happy camper at the Nuremberg war crime trials. He did not apologize to anybody for his horrible role in the war. And the haughty pig was loathe to receive punishment. He literally cheated the hangman by taking cyanide the night before he was to be executed.

Nazis: engineers of evil
unequalled in earth history

In the 1980s, an American college professor gained fame and indignant outrage by publishing a paper that claimed that the Holocaust of World War II was but a myth. According to him, the atrocities never happened. And there were others who stepped forward and attempted to support his theory.

Even a weak attempt to hide the truth of history's most colossal crime against humanity should be labeled a mortal sin. The facts of mankind's darkest years have been extremely well documented – by witnesses, historians...and, survivors.

Adolph Hitler's elaborate plan for eradication of what he considered undesirable elements was in effect only six years - from 1939 through 1945. In that time, his engines of destruction caused the extermination of six-million European Jewish people in 2,000 Nazi concentration and forced-labor camps. An additional six million gypsies, Poles, homosexuals, Jehovah's Witnesses and handicapped were killed in Hitler's bid to purify the earth and create what he termed a "master race."

Obviously, this bizarre endeavor was not pulled off by a mere handful of maniacs. Hundreds of thousands of Germans were party to the massacre. Incredibly, the architects and implementors of the Holocaust were among the Fatherland's elite: Doctors supervised the mass killings and conducted macabre experiments on live subjects, judges stripped Jewish citizens of their rights and possessions and German businessmen gleefully bid on contracts of the crematoriums and German scientists seized upon a perverted and racial Darwinism to justify what they labeled as "genetic purification."

Auschwitz-Birkenau remains the most notorious of the extermination camps. From its opening in March of 1942 until its closing in November of 1944, 1.5 million Jews and tens of thousands of gypsies and Soviet POWs were exterminated. Other noxiously notable camps were Treblinka (opened, July of 1942; closed, August of 1943: 870,000 killed); Chelmno (opened, December of 1941; closed, April of 1943: 320,000 killed); Sobibor (opened, April of 1942; closed, October of 1943: 250,000 killed); Lublin-Majdanek (opened, October of 1941; closed, July of 1944: 360,000 killed) and Belzec (opened, March of 1942; closed, December of 1942: 600,000 killed). In that brief and impossible-to-blot-from-mind period of time, the Nazis also built hundreds of other camps to imprison their peaceful, defensiveless enemies. The network included labor camps, transit camps, prisoner-of-war camps, concentration and extermination camps.

The losses to spouses, parents, children and countries were, indeed, colossal. Poland lost nearly all (3,300,000) of its Jewish population, Slovakia lost over a million, Hungary lost 569,000, Germany lost 141,500, France lost 77, 370, Austria lost 50,000...and so the Nazi Holocaust juggernaut rolled, all across Europe.

The Germans were more obsessed with the extermination of innocent peoples than with winning battles against their adversaries. They continued their horrible extermination carnage until the bitter end. And though U.S. commanders knew about the death camps, they concentrated all efforts on winning the war and ignored opportunities to bomb rail lines leading to the camps and the gas chambers they knew were there.

When the camps were finally liberated, late in 1944, many who witnessed the awfulness were so jolted into shock and scarred that they went into denial and blocked the awful memories from their minds for the rest of their lives.

But the Holocaust did happen. It was an atrocity beyond description. Sadly, the concept of "eye for eye" had never, and will never, be adequately retributed. There can never be satisfaction in Holocaust accountability, nowhere near what should be appropriate. The world did not do its job in the late forties and fifties, when it should have and when it would have been much easier, but it didn't.

Today, 50 years after the Holocaust ended, there are still 1,000 active cases against war criminals around the world. What makes that especially frustrating to Holocaust sympathizers are the facts on how Holocaust retribution was so abysmally conducted right after the crimes were reported to the world at large.

From 1945 through 1990, 102,134 people in Germany were prosecuted in one form or another for war crimes. But authorities have had a ridiculous conviction rate. Only a pathetic six percent, or 6,200 black souls, received punishment. And while some of those were executed, most got off with prison sentences. And 94% got off scot-free. And that figure doesn't even include the thousands who weren't even prosecuted. The barbarism was so massive, chasing war criminals in the reconstruction of Europe after the war was not considered as big an issue as it most certainly should have been. People who killed 50 to 100 prisoners were considered small fry and weren't even hunted down or put on lists to be dealt with later.

Today, most older Germans who were alive during the Holocaust would like to see their national spirit redeemed, while Germany's younger generation considers itself spared of the responsibility of the mass extermination of millions. There's a popular modern saying in Germany today: "To the grace of a late birth."

The atrocities were repugnant, history's main blight on the mores of humanity. That they occurred but 50 years ago, within the lifetimes of so many of us, make them personally revolting. God spare us all from ever returning to such unfathomable behavior.

These frauleins were not fair damsels. *They were bitches who helped butcher millions of innocent people. This photo was taken as American troops liberated the long-suffering holocaust survivors.*

Ten thousand Zeroes
are a lot of zeroes in any language.

That's how many of this particular kind of fighter plane were built by the Japanese for use in World War I, and the legendary Mitsubishi A6M2 Model 21 Zeroes were of such remarkable design that their demise did not come easily. In the very beginning, the odds were totally with the Zeroes. Of course, it was completely one-sided in that surprise 110 - minute attack on Ford Island on Oahu on that fateful Sunday, December 7, 1941, when some 260 Zeroes accounted for 2,403 dead Americans, 1,178 wounded and four sunk battle-ships. It was the near annihilation of America's Pacific Fleet.

Only 29 Zeroes were lost in that first attack. It would take four years of the best of the rest of the world to down the remaining 9,971. The Zero did not possess a particularly powerful engine. There were only 780 horsepower in the proto-type A6M1 and but 1,130 in the final A6M7. To compensate, designer Jiro Horikashi created an incredibly light frame for the Zero. Throughout the war, no plane was the Zero's match in aerobatics. American and British pilots were instructed to never attempt to dogfight the Zero. To overcome the Zero, the Allies chose to build planes with superior speed and power. Also, as the war grew on, the stronger and more durable Hellcats, Wildcats, Lightnings, Sopwith Camels and Spads were far less susceptible to combat damage.

Another factor that gave Zero pilots the edge in the war's beginnings was their near suicidal nature. One of their favorite tactics was to dare to outlive their opponent in head-on passes. And they constantly tried to sucker the Yanks into dogfights, trying to get chasers to climb toward them, at which time they would half roll and come blazing down to become the attackers.

10,000 Japanese Zeroes were built in World War I. Only two, including this one, remain.

Early on, the Zero dominated the Pacific sky. From Oahu to the Marianas to the Solomons to Sumatra and on to New Guinea, the pilots of America, Australia, Holland and England were all greeted with the common performance of a quick, steep climb, into a pirouette turn, and the grand finale: the sudden explosion of on-target cannonfire.

It was this basic maneuver that enabled Zero pilot Hiroyoshi Nishizawa to become Japan's top ace. His score reached 87 kills, double that of America's top ace. The number would have undoubtedly been higher, but Nishizawa met an unfortunate death when a transport in which he hitched a ride was shot down, with no survivors.

Besides the superior planes that came later in the war, much of the credit for figuring out how to beat the Zero goes to Claire Chennault and his American Volunteer Group, the Flying Tigers. One of those Tigers offered this advice to new pilots taking on the Zero for the first time: "When you see them wheeling around, generally above you, slam your throttle through the gate and climb all you can. When they come down, try to dive through them, balls out. Take a shot where you can and keep going in a shallow dive. When you're out of range, pull up and come back at them the same way. Hit and run. If you turn, they'll get you."

Hiroyoshi Nishizawa, *Japan's top ace, was one tough pilot. Other Japan pilots nicknamed him "The Devil.."*

One of the favorite fighter planes of the war was the Grumman F6F Hellcat,
which replaced the Grumman F4F Wildcat in 1943. The Hellcat was strong, durable
and rugged enough to take on the heretofore indomitable Japanese Zero.

What endeared the new Hellcat to crewmen and pilots alike was its remarkable
mechanical reliability. Throughout the remainder of the war, the average of all front-
line Hellcats ready and available for combat was over 90 percent – a record not
matched by any other fighter plane.

Another plane built to beat the Zero was the Chance Vought F4U Corsair, which could lick the Zero in every phase of aerial warfare. It had more speed, more firepower, could climb higher and was more maneuverable in combat. Powered by a 2,000 horse-power Pratt and Whitney engine and with a speed in excess of 400 miles an hour, Corsairs cleared the skies of Zeros nearly every time they engaged in combat with them in the South Pacific, from May of 1943 until the end of the war.

Another of the war's heroes was Commander David McCampbell, the Navy's top ace. On one infamous day, June 19th in 1944, he shot down seven planes. And during the 1944 Battle of Leyte Gulf, which turned out to be the last stand for Japan's carrier forces, Commander McCampbell had an even better day. On that day, October 24, he shot down nine planes.

Marine Top Ace Gregory Boyington was not as fortunate as Commander McCampbell. Boyington flew P-40s with Claire Chennault's Flying Tigers in 1942 and was such a hell-raiser that Chennault grounded him. But he returned to join Chennault's famous "Black Sheep" squadron and flew F43 Corsairs throughout 1943, raising his hit total to 28. Then, early in 1944, during a fighter sweep over Raboul, Boyington's Corsair was hit. He parachuted out and was picked up by a Japanese submarine. Boyington then spent the rest of the war in a Japanese prison.

Among the 10 percent of F6F Hellcats unable to answer the call to duty was this battle-damaged fighter that had this unconventional landing on the USS Essex sometime in 1944.

As soon as Corsairs started reaching Navy pilots in the Pacific, *early in 1944, America started scoring major wins. But Corsair toughness was not aimed only at the Japanese. Even seasoned Navy pilots had a hard time learning to fly the powerful Corsairs. Combat training in them usually took twice as long, and there were, in fact, more Corsairs lost in training than in combat. By the end of 1944, the Corsair had a nickname: the " Bent-wing Eliminator."*

The United States' Top Ace was Dick Bong, who became the first American to top Eddie Rickenbacker's score. He totalled 40 victories in his P-38. Not noted for superior marksmanship and gunnery tactics, Bong compensated with sheer guts. He was not afraid to fly right up next to his targets. When he did break Rickenbacker's record, he was reassigned and made an Advanced Combat Instructor. While taking students on practice flights in the Southwest Pacific, Bong bent the rules and racked up 13 more enemy planes.

The P-38 Lightning was Lockheed's answer to both a design opportunity and an engine shortage. The Army Air Force wanted a better fighter than the P-39 and P-40, but couldn't count on a more powerful engine than those fighters' Allison V -1710s. By putting two Allisons on one light but sturdy airframe, Lockheed got the boost in performance and got into the military aircraft market. During World War II, American pilots destroyed more Japanese aircraft from P-38s than from any other plane.

Pappy Boyington's "Black Sheep" Squadron wasn't the only great black American squadron in the war. The 99th Fighter Squadron was truly black. These were the first black pilots in American military. They were stationed first in Tunisia, then in Sicily and Italy. They flew P-40s, P-39s and P-47s before receiving P-51s in 1944. With three other black squadrons, they formed the 332nd Fighter Group. Their main missions became escorting bombing missions over Germany. They never lost a bomber.

We also had a crack all - black infantry division in the war. *It was the 93rd, shown here marching in a parade at Fort Huachuca, Arizona in the summer of 1943. During the war, the majority of blacks served in segregated supply and construction units, which were not sent into battle. Such was the strangeness of the behavior of our unenlightened leaders in those days.*

Our boys were allowed to take cheesecake overseas.

The Petty Girl,
named after artist George Petty.

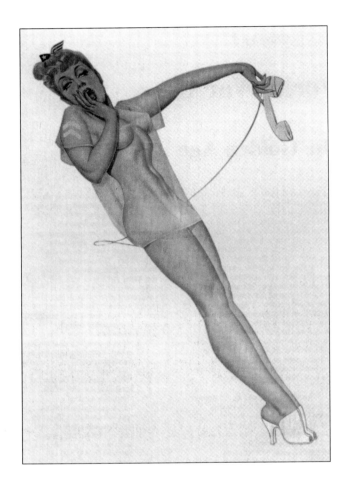

The two things our boys overseas missed most from home were loved ones and lovelies in general. In particular, the lovelies that graced the most barracks walls, foot lockers and aircraft nose cones were Esquire magazine's Petty Girl and the Varga Girl. Millions of magazine gatefolds, calendars and pinup posters were printed for the enjoyment of the troops and hundreds were copied onto aircraft. They also inspired military artists to create their own cuties for the clouds.

The Varga Girl,
named after artist Alberto Vargas.

33

Mrs. 'D' graced this P-47, and was similar to a pinup in the December 1944 Esquire for military personnel.

(below) This B-29 gave the **Tanaka Termite** some 60 rides over enemy targets during World War I.

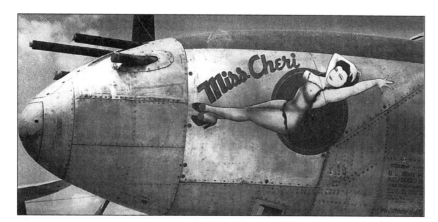

Miss Cheri, shown on this P-38, was based on one of Alberto Vargas' popular Esquire girls.

Cole Porter's movie musical, **Panama Hattie,** was the inspiration for the beauty on this B-17 Flying Fortress.

Audie Murphy, *America's most decorated WWII hero, proudly displays two of the medals he was awarded: the Congressional Medal of Honor (left) and the Legion of Merit. In all, Lieutenant Murphy was awarded over 25 separate citations, including high awards from both France and Belgium.*

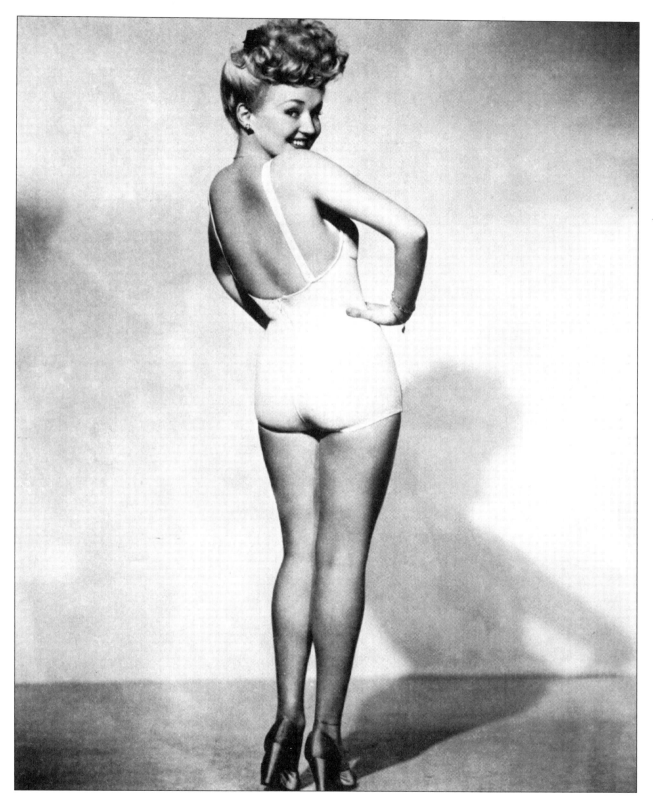

Betty Grable's famous legs decorated locker doors and airplane noses all over Europe and the Pacific all during the war.

The day that the Allies landed on the beaches of Normandy, France, was the day that the tide turned in the second world war in 25 years...the Dow Jones high was 152...unemployment was 1.2% ... a ticket to a broadway show cost $3...a new girdle cost $9...one pound of porterhouse steak required 12 points of precious ration stamps...Marlene Dietrich toured with the USO and sang for the lonely GIs in Italy...and the St. Louis Cardinals beat the St. Louis Browns in the World Series.

The liberation of Paris, 1944

Making Paris ready for Marlene

In the long, illustrious history of the nation of France, the year 1944 went down as one of the most memorable dates. When it opened, the entire country was under the sway of the German army, and when it closed there were relatively few Germans alive on French soil. This seemingly miraculous change from total occupation to almost total liberation began on the morning of June 6, when in the largest armada ever assembled – 250,000 men, 4,000 ships, and 11,000 planes of the forces of Great Britain, Canada and the United States – struck at the coast of Normandy and quickly breached the Germans' Atlantic Wall.

The great Allied landing operation took more than a year of vast preparation. General Eisenhower was sent to London to head SHAEF (Supreme Headquarters Allied Expeditionary Forces). American stores, equipment, and men moved steadily into Britain. Troops were given intensive training for months in landing operations and fighting. The coast defenses of Hitler's "Atlantic Wall" were softened up by continual bombing and airplane raids struck at synthetic oil plants, rail communications and industrial areas in Germany to cripple the Nazi power of resistance.

The most difficult part of the whole undertaking seemed to be the crossing of the English Channel with its stormy waters, swift currents, and 18-foot rise and fall of tide. June 5 was originally fixed as D-Day, but when June 4 was still stormy, Eisenhower decided at midnight to postpone the expedition for 24 hours. If he had postponed it for two weeks until the next "quiet period," his forces would have been ashore in Normandy just on the eve of the Great Storm — one of the worst in 40 years — which swept the beaches from June 19 to 22.

Paris was liberated in August by French and American troops answering the call of patriots fighting the Germans from within. The once gay city was sorrowful, its inhabitants at extremes of near starvation or black-market plenty, defiant resistance or complacent collaboration. Food was the greatest problem, clothing next. The city was not damaged as much as had been feared. Retreating Germans set fire to the surrounding military forts. A wing of the Versailles Palace was burned and there was heavy damage to the Luxemburg Gardens, as the Germans made their last stand in these buildings.

By the time the last German was finally evicted, the old city was already well on the road to recovery. You could hear singing again and visitors quickly discovered that the Nazis hadn't found all the wine and champagne.

For Marlene Dietrich, the timing could not have been better.

Lili Marlene
in the Battle of the Bulge

History best remembers Marlene Dietrich for many things. This Berlin-born femme fatale first revealed her mysterious sexiness and sultry cabaret singing voice in the German film The Blue Angel in 1930. It made her an instant international sensation. By 1933, she was renting the Hearst beach mansion in California. Her lovers included the Frenchman Maurice Chevalier. Her talent was limitless, and her movies were but romantic chapters of her real life: Shanghai Express, Blonde Venus, Song of Songs, The Scarlet Empress. In Blonde Venus, she played these roles: hausfrau, mother, fallen angel, whore, successful nightclub entertainer - while introducing the world to a newcomer she thought could someday become a star: Cary Grant.

When **Marlene Dietrich** arrived in Europe, the USO never looked so good to U.S. troops.

The GIs of World War II remember Marlene Dietrich, too, for in 1944 Marlene went a-soldiering. She joined the USO and with a young comic named Danny Thomas left New York's La Guardia airport in the middle of a hailstorm on April 14: destination unknown. After refueling stops in Greenland and the Azores, her troupe landed at Casablanca and then finally arrived in Algiers some four days later, where they did their first show. One of her opening lines, as she gazed into the starstruck eyes of a teenage soldier, was: "When a GI looks at me, it's not too hard to read his mind."

Between shows, Marlene toured hospital wards, singing or just visiting. Raising morale was the primary goal of USO entertainers. As were so many women civilians and entertainers of the USO, she was fearless, heroic and dedicated. Because she was Marlene Dietrich, the laurels she collected for her heroic bravery were medals, citations, devotion and respect.

By the time her troupe got to Italy, she had picked up an accordionist, a Texas comedienne and another comic and the inscription on the back of her helmet read: "To the sweetheart of the American Army. A swell G.I., Hqrts. 34th Inf. Div. Italy, 1944." On the 6th of June, 1944, Marlene announced the news of the Normandy invasion to an audience of nearly 4,000 GIs.

In September, she was on her way to France. Through connections, she managed to be brought to the personal attention of one of her heroes, the flamboyant, pistol-packing General George Patton. She stayed attached to Patton's Third Army. She loved this brash soldier, his bravado and his military arrogance. And he, in turn, basked in her utter devotion and kept her as close to him as possible, until orders separated them in December.

The USO meets more brass: General Omar Bradley. According to her diary, Omar was afraid of Marlene.

According to Marlene's diary, she was in the Ardennes, at Bastogne, when the Germans surrounded the American forces to which she was attached, which included the 101st Airborne Division under the command of General Anthony McAuliffe. When German General Luttwitz asked for the Americans to surrender, he got back the now famous reply of McAuliffe, "Nuts!" That reply did two things. It confused the Germans, because they couldn't interpret it. And it raised the morale of the American troops to the extent that certain defeat was no longer a certainty.

In the middle of this battle that historians later dubbed The Battle of the Bulge, it became apparent that Marlene Dietrich and her troupe needed rescuing. And as Marlene sat there on the cold ground, coughing and waiting in the snow, she looked up to see an American Flying Fortress, from whose hatch came the paratroopers of the 82nd Airborne Division. And the first of these was none other than General James M. Gavin, a man who quickly replaced George Patton as Marlene Dietrich's favorite general.

"Hi there, soldier!"

It is said that Jumpin' Jim Gavin brought Marlene safely back to Paris in his Jeep - not on a white horse - then left her. How this was done under USO regulations was never checked, but it's so romantic, who cares?

Marlene was put up at the Ritz, newly redecorated in this newly liberated city. The diary never says what happened to the troupe's accordionist, Texas comedienne and comic - but we can assume they made it out safely, too.

Some people even look sharp in un-dress military.

Marlene meets **General Jumpin' Jim Gavin.**

The lady did know how to draw crowds, war or no war.

Marlene with pal **General George S. Patton, Jr.**

One corporal's memories
from World War II

When Leonard A. Hacker was inducted into the Army on October 10, 1942, he left the gold hills of Calaveras County, California with one dread. Leonard had never flown in an airplane, and never wanted to - the thought of flying made him ill. After basic training, he was placed in the Army Air Force and flew all over the world. When the war was ending, he was in Europe and got a horrible, first-hand look at the horrors of the holocaust. That made him more ill than he'd ever been in his life.

When Leonard died, in 1992, these photographs were found in a small box. It was the first his family knew that Leonard had been to the Nazi extermination camps. The sights he saw were so horrifying, he never spoke of them. The small, faded pictures are reprinted here to show once again the unholy insanity of the Nazi scourge.

Corporal Hacker *is the tall soldier on the left.*

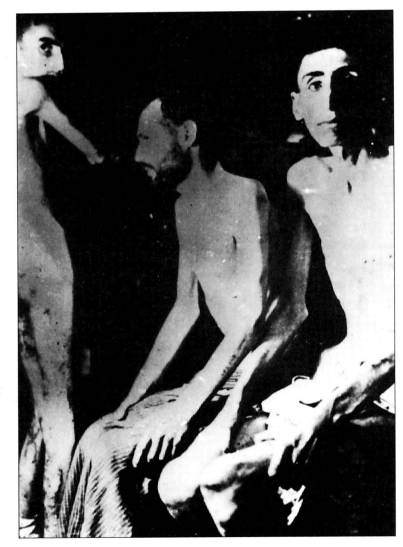

The Not To Be Forgotten Forties

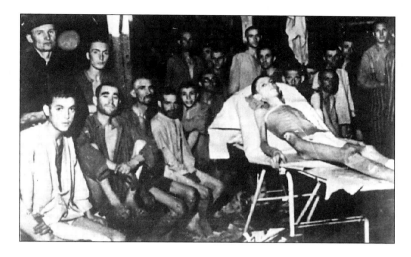

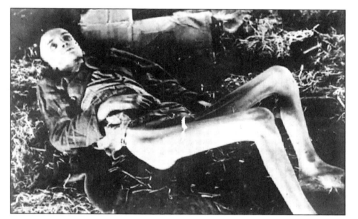

Where did all the Japanese-Americans go?

Sad to say, they were all deported to "relocation camps." That was the first tragedy. The second was when bureaucratic hangups kept them there for two and a half years.

In February of 1944, the War Relocation Authority, the agency created to take charge of relocating 110,000 Japanese-Americans living on the Pacific coast, was transferred to the Department of Interior.

Ten months later, On December 17, Major General H. Conger Pratt, Western Commander, issued a proclamation that ended the 30-month exclusion of the 110,000 men, women and children of Japanese ancestry from the states of California, Washington and Oregon. His order, to be effective on January 2, 1945, was upheld by the United States Supreme Court.

Japanese students were admitted to American colleges and universities again and the young men of eligible age were included in the national draft as well as being permitted to enlist in the armed services. And a final chapter of glorious irony was recorded by the 100th Battalion. Made up almost entirely of Japanese from the Hawaiian Islands, this battalion won distinction for its fighting at Cassino.

Conditions at the relocation centers *did not remind the Japanese Americans of home. They were awful.*

In the Pacific, conditions were much, much worse.

By 1945, the once tranquil islands of the Pacific were horribly reshaped by the scars of war. Beaches were littered with corpses and bomb craters became foxholes as the Marines moved onto island after island.

One by one, the islands of the Pacific were taken by U.S. troops and names of tiny patches of land like Guadalcanal, Kolombangara, Bougainville, Tarawa, Makin, the Marshalls, Kwajalein, Palau, Guam, Tinian, the Marianas, Leyte, Luzon, Ormoc, Mindoro, Corregidor, Iwo Jima and Okinawa became indelibly stamped in the pages of world history.

On February 19, 1945, the U.S. Marines landed on Iwo Jima. Four days later, Mt. Suribachi was captured. This panorama shows the Third Marine Division encamped on the southeast edge of Motoyama Airfield No. One, covering the beach area of Mt. Suribachi to the east boat basin.

This photograph was taken the day Mt. Suribachi was captured, on February 23, 1945.

The Marines landed on Guam on July 21, 1944. Marine infantry, supported by tanks, took three weeks of heavy fighting to defeat the 19,000 defenders of Guam. This unfortunate soul was among that number.

The fighting was brutal and casualties were immense on both sides. On Leyte, 80,000 Japanese soldiers were killed.

The U.S. Marines landed on Iwo Jima on February 19, 1945, and captured Mount Suribachi four days later. And this picture became the most famous image of the most colossal war in history.

The Kamikaze Missions
American anti-aircraft gunners shooting to stay alive
vs.
Japanese pilots diving to die

What mind could get so warped to ask a country's children to die for a hopeless cause? What culture could be so crazed to create children willing gladly to comply to such a bizarre charge? Sadly, this was the condition that existed in the waning months of the war, when Japan was so desperate that air missions of suicide became a final hope for victory.

One example of this horrible era of sacrifice because of insanity occurred on Iwo Jima, when island garrison commander General Kuribayashi sent his last message to Tokyo, informing Nippan hierarchy that he had exhausted all ammunition and the last drop of water. Rather than surrender, the general shot himself while most of his men fought to their deaths.

Fortunately for these young fanatics, the war ended before they were old enough to get involved. By the final days of the war, Japanese military strategists were enlisting students to fly kamikaze planes. For the glory of the Rising Sun, kamikaze kids were sent on one-way flights to their death.

The war was then entering its final desperate phase. But a choice of suicide was a contradiction to the essence of the Japanese philosophy of Bushido. Supposedly, it was out of the question for any Japanese soldier to surrender without a struggle. One was expected to fight on until one's sword was broken and one's last arrow spent. But this was a paradox born of lunacy. Generals were allowed to shoot themselves in the head, while Japanese children and soldiers were asked to die in battle.

The first kamikaze attack occurred in October of 1944, when there was little left of the once mighty Japanese navy and air force. Two frustrated and fanatical pilots turned their planes into bombs and tried to strike enemy ships, one a giant carrier. Though they both missed, the Japanese were inspired and likened the acts to Shimpu, the divine wind which had spared the Japanese a Mongul conquest seven centuries earlier. How Shimpu got interpreted as kamikaze is due to the fact that all Japanese characters have a double pronunciation. The Nisei (American servicemen of Japanese ancestry) of the U.S. forces did not know how to read Japanese correctly and translated the term in its vernacular way rather than the dignified and solemn version.

The 201st Fighter Squadron of the 1st Naval Air Fleet formed Japan's first kamikaze attack corps. Originally, they didn't intend on suicide missions. Fighters were chosen because, for every bomber in Japanese production, five fighter planes could be built. Loaded with a 550-pound bomb, the fighters would become bombers. This bizarre idea was dreamed up by none less than the pilots of those fighter planes. At first, they thought they could drop the bombs. But after study and training, physics worked against that notion. If the pilots wave-hopped their planes and skipped the bombs toward their target (that's right; bounced them off the surface of the sea) they would have to fly so low that the pilots would become victims of their own explosions. Normal tactics were no longer valid. Crashing the fighters against the aircraft carriers became the final resort. This notion was proposed directly to the pilots, not their squadron leaders, by Japanese Vice Admiral Onishi. Strangely, almost to a man, the pilots gladly accepted the assignments.

After the navy, the Japanese army adopted the kamikaze method of attacking enemy warships. During the Battle of the Philippines, the army lost 658 men on suicide missions. In the Battle for Leyte, between November of 1944 and January of 1945, at least six major Allied ships were sunk or damaged by kamikaze raids with a loss of hundreds of lives. During the landing of American forces on Luzon, kamikaze activity was in full fury. Japan's most prestigious warplanes - Zeroes, Kates, Vals, Shidens and Suiseis - were wasted daily. When the war got to Okinawa, thousands of kamikaze attacks (actual count: 2,571) were flown, resulting in 13 sunk ships and 174 damaged. The suicide pilots were not kept informed of these results, which did little to change the course of the war.

Nearly 4,000 Japanese pilots died in kamikaze missions. Vice Admiral Onishi appeased his conscience by committing hari kari on August 16, 1945.

One of the kamikaze planes that didn't make it to the target was this Yokosaka Model 33 that crashed just short of an American carrier.

The U.S.S. Bunker Hill was one of the American carriers disemboweled by the kamikazes.

The final blow for freedom

On August 9, 1945, the U.S. dropped this atomic bomb on Nagasaki, Japan. It was but three days after the first atomic bomb devastated Hiroshima. The bomb was labeled "Little Boy" and weighed 10,000 pounds and carried the equivalent of 20,000 tons of high explosive.

- **On August 10,** Japan offered its surrender.

- **On August 14,** Japan agreed to unconditional surrender.

- **On August 15,** the day forever forth known as VJ Day, Japan's Emperor Hirohito announced surrender to the Japanese people.

- **On August 28,** U.S. troops landed on Japanese soil.

- **On September 2,** the Japanese signed formal surrender papers on the USS Missouri.

- **On September 8,** General Douglass MacArthur arrived in Tokyo to assume control of the occupation.

- **On September 9,** the Japanese surrendered in China.

- **On September 12,** the Japanese surrendered all forces in Southeast Asia.

- **On September 16,** the Japanese surrendered in Hong Kong.

At the time, it was universally believed that the bomb to end all bombing had officially ended the war to end all wars. Unfortunately, the world once again proved to have a very short memory.

After they plundered humanity, they tried to cheat the hangman.

Japanese General Kuribayashi, garrison commander at Iowa Jima, met his maker on his own terms. He shot himself in the head.

Japanese Vice Admiral Onishi, the man responsible for Japan's kamikaze missions, committed hari kari.

German Chancellor Adolph Hitler and his mistress, Eva Braun, ended their time on earth living in sin by committing suicide on May 1, 1945.

German Luftwaffe chief Hermann Goering went on trial at Nuremberg in November of 1945, along with 21 other Nazis, including Hess, Ribbentrop, Speer, Jodl, Keitel, Raeder and Doenitz. Most shocking testimony was delivered by Rudolf Hess, former commandant of Auschwitz, who delivered a calm recital of nearly two-million murders. Hess was sentenced to life imprisonment but committed suicide. Goering, who remained an unrepentant Nazi to the end, cheated the hangman by taking cyanide on the eve of his execution.

Benito Mussolini, leader of Fascist Italy, celebrated few successes in the war. His navy could not even control the Mediterranean. He was overthrown in 1943 and rescued from partisans by German troops under Otto Skorzeny. Mussolini probably would have committed suicide, but the public nailed him first. Italian partisans assassinated Benito and his mistress on April 28, 1945, then hanged them upside down in a public square in Milan. The corpses were then dragged across Italy behind a donkey cart to make it possible for thousands of Italians to come up and spit on them.

Japanese Prime Minister Hideki Tojo, realizing his inadequacies as a war leader, tried to commit suicide. He bungled that, too. He was convicted of war crimes by the Allies in 1946 and was hanged on December 23, 1948.

Karl Adolf Eichmann, Reichssicherheitshaputamt manager of Department IV 4b, was in charge of the extermination of European Jews - the "Final Solution" decided upon at the Wansee conference in Berlin. At the end of the war, Eichmann escaped to Argentina. He was kidnapped by Israeli agents in 1960, sent to Israel and put on trial. He was hanged.

Benito Mussolini and his mistress *did not escape the hangman. Their fellow Italians demonstrated their dislike for the illustrious pair by displaying their corpses upside down in this public square in Milan.*

Yalta was neither Roosevelt's nor Churchill's finest hour.

To fully appreciate what happened at the February, 1945, meeting of "The Big Three" at Yalta in the Crimea to determine the shape of postwar Europe and to gain Soviet help for the final campaigns to subdue Japan, one must go all the way back to the end of World War I. That's when a profoundly disturbing trend in human affairs began.

At the end of the first world war, America elected to isolate itself and have as little as possible to do with warring countries. Britain was so wounded by that war, it needed decades of healing. Conquest was not an ambition of either of these powers. Such was not the case in Soviet Russia.

Winston Churchill, a weary Franklin Roosevelt and Joseph Stalin *pose for posterity at Yalta in February, 1945.*

Between World War I and II, Germany, Italy and Japan were not the only super powers to develop totalitarian regimes based on greed, personal gain and conquest of other nations. In fact, long before those powers embarked on their revolutions, Russia was hard at it. Despite Russian propaganda to the contrary, the Bolshevik seizure of power in Russia in November of 1917 was not a great popular revolution. Dates often get misplaced in history. The tyrannical Russian Tsars were overthrown by decent peoples in March of 1917. These were men who believed in liberal democracy very similar to the politics of America and Britain. But they were no match for the small group of revolutionaries who called themselves Bolsheviks who overthrew them in November. The Bolsheviks were implacably opposed to western-style democracy, and the tyranny that followed under their rule was far worse than anything the Russians had known under the tsars.

The leader of this band of fanatics was one Vladimir Ilyich Ulyanov. He called himself Lenin. You know from pictures what an odd-looking duck he was. He had Asiatic origins, disguised by beady eyes and high cheekbones. He was also short, stout, balding and had a dome-shaped head and wore a pointy beard. And he was meaner than he looked.

Lenin had one goal in life: power. Everything he did was calculated to that end. He had no social graces nor conscience. No trace of idealism, no smattering of moral scruple came between Lenin and his lust for power. His partner in atrocities of the future was another mean-looking bundle of evil, a squat-shaped organizer named Lev Davidovich Bronstein. He called himself Trotsky.

Lenin interpreted the theories of Karl Marx to suit his diabolical needs and then he and Trotsky pulled off the Bolshevik Revolution with a gang of but 5,000 thugs. Amazingly, it was a small group at the outset and remained that way for over 75 years. It was a small clique of men and women determined to seek power by any means and hold on to it at any cost - even if it meant the destruction of Russia, or even the world.

And where was Joseph Vissarionovich Dzhugashvili while all this purging and revolutionizing was going on? And who was he? That would be the infamous Joseph Stalin.

He had but recently returned from five years' exile in Siberia, where he had been sentenced for, among other crimes, organizing bank raids to finance his friends in the Georgian underground. Stalin returned to take over the editorship of Pravda, the publication which translates, oddly, to "Truth."

From these three crooks came the foundation of Russia's Communist Party. It came to power by force and remained in power by force. Lenin set up a totalitarian police state and it essentially remained unchanged from the form he gave it for over 75 years. And the repression that Russians and, eventually Chinese, Yugoslavs, Hungarians, Koreans and Germans would endure under communism would make life under the old tsars seem like heaven on earth.

Though Stalin played a minor role in the revolution, he did catch up quickly. In 1920, Lenin honestly believed that world revolution was imminent. He convinced Stalin of this, and Joe went to work. He managed to get himself appointed Secretary-General to the Communist Party, and set about bringing all party organizations under his personal control. When Lenin died, in 1924, Stalin overwhelmed Trotsky in a classic power play and had Trotsky exiled to his former prison, Siberia. He then had Trotsky deported from the USSR in 1929, and had Trotsky murdered in Mexico on his orders, in 1940.

From the 1920s on, world revolution was Stalin's intent. By the 1930s, he had eliminated all the old Bolshevik leaders. Communism was his to run and would be the instrument with which he would rule the world.

By any standards, Stalin was an atrocious ruler of humanity. He starved his countrymen to equip his soldiers for war. Then he starved the soldiers, too. He refused to sign the Hague Convention agreement on prisoners of war or to pay contributions to the International Red Cross. Due to his incompetence, hundreds of thousands of Russian soldiers were captured in the first Nazi attack on the Soviet Union. Abandoned by Stalin, they suffered a horrible fate in German prison camps. Many had surrendered because it beat the alternative: starvation. After the war, when German armies withdrew from Russian territory, whole divisions of anti-Stalin Russian forces were found among the German armies, including Cossack regiments. These anti-Stalin Russians had fought, and defeated, the Red Army in battles right up to the end of the war. Some six-million Russian nationalists were left stranded in Germany, and Stalin wanted them back - to work in his labor camps in the Arctic Circle. He would condemn their leaders to torture and execution.

Everyone at Yalta knew about all this, including Churchill and Roosevelt. But Churchill agreed secretly that the stranded Russians would be repatriated. And they were. They were brutally forced into vehicles, ships and trains for handing over to Soviet authorities. Many committed suicide rather than fall into Stalin's hands. Many were marched straight from disembarkation points in the Crimea to execution yards. All told, Stalin murdered tens of millions of people whom communist law condemned as "enemies of the people."

As hideous as he was, Hitler wasn't the biggest rat in the war. Stalin was. But Stalin did not limit his wrath to his countrymen. Of the 90 - thousand German soldiers captured at Stalingrad, only five thousand ever made it back to the Fatherland. History has lost records of what happened to the missing 85 thousand.

This then was the political pig Churchill and Roosevelt had to deal with at Yalta.

Why they were so compliant to Stalin will forever be a mystery. In this three-handed game of world politics, the leaders of democracy held the aces. Had it not been for a colossal blunder by Hitler, Russia probably would have lost its war with Germany. Russian citizens, in fact, welcomed the Germans as liberators from the Lenin-Stalin regime. Had Hitler pursued that role, they would have gained Russian support. But Hitler was not that smart. His Nazi troops were so brutal, the Russian people turned on them, too.

Both Churchill and Roosevelt knew, at Yalta, that communism had already failed. Yet they both succeeded in helping to bequeath it 50 more years of repression and horror. They reckoned that Yalta was not the time to denounce Stalin or communism. After all, it was their propaganda that had transformed Stalin as a big-hearted, big-muscled friend of the western Alliance.

Churchill should have been smarter. Roosevelt had an excuse. He was so crippled by the time he arrived at Yalta, he literally had but weeks to live. Only his towering ego kept him alive through the proceedings. Churchill did have a private meeting with Roosevelt to warn him of Stalin's ways, but Roosevelt laughed him off. Other men had warned him about communism, and he had laughed them off, too.

Yalta was a strange mishmash of personalities. Roosevelt was not only naive and overmatched, he was seriously deranged. He was more jealous of Churchill than concerned about Stalin and communism. Churchill, on the other hand, was appalled by his ally, Roosevelt, and held Stalin in awe. At his first meeting with Stalin, in 1942, Churchill turned to the British Ambassador in Moscow and said, "I want that man to like me." Why? Well, even great men aren't always perfect.

The Yalta meeting lasted seven days. Bizarre things happened in that week. At one point, Roosevelt goaded Stalin into proposing a toast to the execution of 50,000 German officers. Churchill, to his credit, refused to drink "to such a monstrous toast." Then Churchill delivered his own toast. To Stalin! "...we regard Marshal Stalin's life as most precious to the hopes and hearts of us all...I walk through this world with greater courage and hope when I find myself in a relation of friendship and intimacy with this great man whose fame has gone out not only all over Russia, but the world."

From all accounts of Yalta, it is clear that Churchill and Roosevelt came to bargain with the tyrant Stalin - in the very shadows of his torture chambers and execution yards. And as Nazism crumbled, communism took its place. The siege of Berlin was denied American General George Patton and Britain's Field Marshal Montgomery. They held back as diseased and dirty Soviet soldiers plundered and literally raped the city. And before the war officially ended, Soviet forces were installed in Poland, Bulgaria, Rumania and Hungary. And Germany itself was divided by a wall.

Just two months after Yalta, on April 12, 1945, President Roosevelt died. His successor, Harry Truman, had not been kept informed about governmental policy. His only knowledge of Europe was as an artillery officer in World War I.

The next day, the Red Army captured Vienna, capital of Austria. And the world mourned the death of a great man. But it was not his, nor Churchill's, finest hour.

World War II officially ended on September 2, 1945 *aboard the USS Missouri. Here, American Fleet Admiral Chester W. Nimitz signs the surrender agreement with the Japanese. Behind him, from left to right, are General MacArthur, Admiral William P. Halsey and Rear Admiral Forrest P. Sherman, Chief of Staff for Admiral Nimitz. Six days later, MacArthur arrived in Tokyo to assume control of the occupation.*

55

When World War II ended, the Cold War began.

After the two colossal bomb bangs at Hiroshima and Nagasaki, the war finally ended with millions of people in Europe and Japan either dead or exhausted. It took six years and one day to annihilate as much of the world as nearly possible. Adolph Hitler and Hermann Goering were dead from suicide, Hideki Tojo would soon be slated for the hangman's noose. Some of the evil war criminals would be tried, convicted and put to death later. Others escaped to wage future wars.

The Soviet Union, because of its size and alliance with America and Great Britain, emerged victorious as did the United States, the only power not bombarded on home soil. But, as early as 1946, as Winston Churchill noted in his famous "Iron Curtain" speech, a growing enmity existed between the two super powers. Relations between East and West went from bad to awful as the Soviet Union quickly moved to consolidate its hold on eastern Europe and refused to release its stronghold in Germany. When the Soviet Union blockaded Berlin in 1948, the United States refused to withdraw and airlifted Berlin's supplies for more than a year.

With the presence of nuclear weaponry, cold relations between the Soviets and the United States resulted in an ever tense war of mind and will - until June of 1960, when hostilities between East and West flared in what became the Korean War. The schism would last 40 more years, four long decades of uneasy peace and periodic confrontation. It was a Cold War that got extremely hot as the survivors of Korea and Viet Nam will surely testify.

After 40 long years of arms races on earth and space races above, the Soviet Union showed signs up giving up on communism. In 1989, Hungary and East Germany opened their borders to the free world, allowing for the downfall of communist rule in eastern Europe and an effective conclusion to the Cold War. In 1990, World War II also officially ended with the signing of a peace treaty that finally acknowledged the reunification of Germany.

The Soviets liberated the survivors of the Auschwitz camp on January 26, 1945. The Americans were the first to find the horrors at the Landsberg camp, near Munich. A chamber of horrors greeted General Patton's Third Army at Buchenwald. And when British troops arrived at Belsen, they captured the three goons pictured below.

Peter Weingartner, SS guard.

Hildegarde Lohbauer, SS guard.

Martha Linke, SS guard.

Of the 68 nations involved in WWII, 23 waited until it was nearly over to choose sides.

- **Argentina** declared war on both Germany and Japan on March 27, 1945.

- **Brazil** declared war on Germany and Italy in 1942 but waited until June 6, 1945 to declare war on Japan.

- **Bulgaria** declared neutrality on August 26, 1944, then declared war on Germany 12 days later. Two months later, the Bulgarians severed relations with Japan.

- **Chile** declared war on Japan on April 11, 1945.

- **Egypt** waited until February 24, 1945 to declare war on Germany and Japan.

- **Finland** declared war on Germany on March 3, 1945.

- **Hungary** didn't wait; it switched. The Hungarians first declared war on the Soviet Union and the United States in 1941, then signed an armistice with the Allies on January 20, 1945 and declared war on Germany.

- **Iran** declared war on Germany on September 9, 1943 and on Japan on March 1, 1945.

- **Italy** declared war on France and the United Kingdom and invaded Greece in 1940. Then, in 1941, the Italians declared war on Yugoslavia, the Soviet Union, Cuba and Guatemala. After an unconditional surrender to the Allies on September 8, 1943, they declared war on Germany a month later. On July 14, 1945, they declared war on Japan.

- **Lebanon** declared war on both Germany and Japan on February 27, 1944.

- **Liberia** beat Lebanon by a month, declaring war on Germany and Japan on January 27, 1944.

- **Paraguay** declared war on Germany and Japan on February 7, 1945.

- **Peru** declared war on Germany and Japan on February 12, 1945.

- **Romania** declared war on Germany on August 25, 1944, then on Hungary on September 7, 1944 and then on Japan on March 7, 1945.

- **San Marino** declared war on Germany and Japan on March 1, 1945.

- **Saudi Arabia** declared war on Germany and Japan on March 1, 1945.

- **Sweden** severed relations with Germany on May 7, 1945.

- **Syria** declared war on Germany and Japan on February 26, 1945.

- **Thailand** had trouble making up its mind. Thailand declared war on the United States and the United Kingdom on January 25, 1942, then voided that declaration on August 16, 1945.

- **Turkey** declared war on Germany and Japan on February 23, 1945.

- **The Soviet Union** invaded Poland and Finland in 1939, then got invaded by Germany and Romania in 1941. In 1944, the Russians invaded Romania, Poland, Bulgaria, Yugoslavia and Hungary. In 1945, they invaded Germany. On August 8, 1945, they declared war on already-beaten Japan.

- **Uruguay** waited until February 15, 1945 to declare war on Germany and Japan.

- **Venezuela** joined Uruguay in declaring war on Germany and Japan on February 15, 1945.

Audie Murphy. America's most decorated war hero was awarded over 25 separate citations, including the Congressional Medal of Honor, the Legion of Merit and high awards from both France and Belgium.

Winston Spencer Churchill. Here was a man whose time had come. Churchill took over as Britain's Prime Minister in the dark days of 1940 and quickly became the proud and stubborn symbol of British defiance against Nazi Germany.

Dwight David Eisenhower. Supreme Allied Commander, then president of the United States.

Baron Carl Gustaf von Mannerheim. He commanded the Finnish army in the futile war with Russia in 1939-40. The Finns lost that one, but did get a chance to retaliate. A couple of years later, Mannerheim's Finnish Army Group joined forces with Germany and they invaded Russia. Obviously, they didn't rack up a conquest. But the Finns did appreciate Mannerheim's resilience. After the war, they elected him president of the country.

Josef Stalin. First, he successfully got away with a name change. He was originally known as Josip Djugashvili, having been born with that monicker. Figuring Joe and Stalin would be easier for history to remember, he then went out and did things to be remembered by. Upon becoming Soviet dictator, he took his Red Army into Finland and almost got more than he bargained for. In 1940, the Finns destroyed Russia's 44th Division on the outskirts of Suomussalmi and then had the courage to send troops on skis after Russian tanks. After this dismal start, Stalin did manage to remain in charge for the remainder of the war, end up on the winning side and cause great consternation to the rest of world afterwards. One of history's really bad guys.

The Supermarine Spitfire. This fighter plane was one of the truly great heroes of the war. Without it, the Battle of Britain would have had a much different outcome. Over 20,000 Spitfires were built and used by the British, Russians and Americans in WWII.

Germany's Panzer Division and the Blitzkrieg Concept, as designed by General Heinz Guderian, were the strength of the German army. Guderian was a great commander and established his credentials early in the war. In April of 1940, his XIX Panzer Korps busted through French defenses near Sudan, causing the defeat of Ango-French forces. To his credit, Heinz did not get along with Adolph; panzer successes were because of him, not the Fuhrer. If the rest of the Nazi army had been as good as Guderian's Panzer Divisions, we might well be goose-stepping around America today.

Isoroku Yamamoto. He was the Commander in Chief of the Japanese combined fleet and designed the attack on Pearl Harbor. He later led the Imperial Navy at the Coral Sea and Midway. He was a game warrior, but realistic. He warned Tojo that Japan could not hang in for a long war. He was killed in action when intercepted by American fighters in April of 1943.

Civilians, especially Soviet civilians. Sadly, nearly eight - million Soviet civilians were killed in the war.

Sumner Welles. Sumner was a good pal of Franklin Roosevelt, close enough for Roosevelt to name him Under Secretary of State. In February of 1940, Welles was sent on a grand tour of London, Rome, Berlin and Paris to negotiate an end to the fighting in Europe.

Wang Ching-wei. Wang was a Chinese fellow who was educated in Japan. In the thirties, he was an adroit waffler. First he would work for the Chinese, then the Japanese, then the Chinese. He was an early disciple of Sun Yat-sen and a leader of the Kuomintang, where he teamed up with Chian Kai-shek. When Japan invaded China and appeared headed for victory, Wang defected back to the Japanese. He was appointed puppet ruler of China by the Japanese army. When the Japanese surrendered to China in 1945, Wang's waffling career was over.

Benito Mussolini. This blustering boob had dreams of establishing a new Holy Roman Empire and sold fellow Italians on that concept to become head of the Fascist party in 1922. His army did not do well in World War II and his navy did worse. It did not rule the seas; it could not, in fact, control the Mediterranean. Benny's fellow Italians overthrew him in 1943 and German troops saved him from those dismayed and irate folks. Two years later, they got him. Italian partisans assassinated him on April 28, 1945 and he was then paraded upside down on a donkey cart across northern Italy, where he was spat on by the populace.

Vidkun Quisling. Here was a traitor who picked the wrong side. He did the paper work that made Norway's surrender to Germany official. He was sentenced to death and shot.

Karl Adolph Eichmann. This was the man in charge of the hideous Holocaust. Officially, he ran Department IV 4b of the Reichssicherheitshaputamt. When the war ended, he escaped to Argentina and managed to elude authorities for 15 years. Justice prevailed in 1960, when Israeli agents kidnapped him and sent to Israel to stand trial. He was convicted, of course, and then hanged.

What WWII cost in lives:

ALLIED CASUALTIES

Soviet Union
Killed - 20.13 million
Wounded - 14 million

China
Killed - 1.32 million
Wounded - 1.76 million

Poland
Killed - 664 thousand
Wounded - 530 thousand

United States
Casualties - 292 thousand
Wounded - 671 thousand

France
Killed in action - 201 thousand
Dead, other causes - 261 thousand
Wounded - 400 thousand

Yugoslavia
Casualties - 730 thousand

United Kingdom
Killed - 357 thousand
Wounded - 369 thousand

Australia
Casualties - 208 thousand

India
Casualties - 96 thousand

Canada
Casualties - 86 thousand

Greece
Casualties - 64 thousand

AXIS CASUALTIES

Germany

Military casualties - 3.26 million
Civilian casualties - 3.35 million
Military wounded - 7.25 million

Japan
Military casualties - 1.27 million
Military wounded - 4.62 million
Military missing - 85 thousand
Civilian casualties - 241 thousand
Civilians wounded - 313 thousand

Austria
Casualties - 280 thousand
Wounded - 350 thousand

Italy
Casualties - 150 thousand
Wounded - 67 thousand
Missing - 135 thousand

Rumania
Casualties - 350 thousand

Hungary
Casualties - 237 thousand

What WWII cost in dollars:

- **The United States** spent $341 billion.

- **The Soviet Union** spent $192 billion.

- **The United Kingdom** spent $120 billion.

- **Germany** spent $272 billion.

- **Italy** spent $94 billion.

- **Japan** spent $56 billion.

- **China and France** spent too much to count.

- **The smaller nations** involved spent another $50 million.

The Not To Be Forgotten Forties

We started the forties on a resurgence from a long depression, isolated from the rest of the world and determined to remain that way. Our factories were making cars and tractors; television and computers were just around the corner. Then, we had to go to war. And in two short years, both women and men were working in our factories making tanks and guns and bombs and ships and planes. And we all sacrificed. And within four years, the world saw our might. And to win back our peace, we gave up some of the best years of our lives and also, indeed, many of our best people.

Women aircraft workers *were in charge of the final inspection of new transparent noses for deadly A-20 attack bombers used for hedge hopping and strafing of enemy ground troops and installations. More women were employed to arm these bombers with light and heavy caliber guns.*

Just ask **Ginger Rogers** how long ago 1940 was. Why, it was just like yesterday. Ginger was starting her 15th year in show business and was already famous for all those musicals with Fred Astaire. And she was about to win her first Oscar, for her 1940 performance in the picture Kitty Foyle. Five years later, she became Hollywood's highest paid star. Sure, she looked a bit more glamorous then. But really, girls...1940 wasn't that far back.

Yeah! It's not ancient history we're talking about here.

Granted, Chicago was barely over 100 years old. And the Civil War had only been over 75 years. And there were still a lot of oldtimers walking around who remembered things like the Spanish American War and the Great Alaskan Gold Rush. And some people (lots, actually) still had outdoor plumbing and not too many knew what television was.

But ancient? Hey, easy now.

There were a few TV sets in the country. They just stopped making bunches because the factories were churning out bullets and tanks.

And didn't FDR fly to Casablanca for that big meeting on a Pan American Clipper across the war-ravaged Atlantic in record time? Hey, modern transportation was here!

Admittedly, some colossal atrocities did sneak up on us. We did sort of stand by stupidly as Joseph Stalin killed nine million to 25 million people in purges. That's before he led the USSR through World War II, in which 21.5 million Soviets died (combined deaths suffered by America, Britain, and France: 1.2 million).

But we were at war against Hitler and the idiots with him who were responsible for the holocaust that took six million more lives. We did everything we could to prevent that, and finally, we did stop it.

That war woke us up. Our allies wanted assurances that America would not again revert to isolationism, repeating our blunder after World War I. In April of 1943, the Associated Press found only 24 senators willing to endorse U.S. participation in a postwar "international peace force." But the American public felt otherwise. After the results of a Gallup poll two weeks later were announced, in which 74% of the public was in favor, a majority of lawmakers caught up with the people they were leading. Resolutions supporting a U.S. role in what would become the United Nations two years later passed the House by 360 to 29 and the Senate by 85 to 5. To the diehards, the *New Yorker* had this to say: "Gentlemen, if you do not know that your country is entangled beyond recall with the rest of the world, what do you know?"

The war helped America find its conscience. When whites fought helmet to helmet with blacks in foreign foxholes, they came back home with different attitudes. It was not until 1947 that Jackie Robinson, a grandson of a slave, broke the major league baseball color barrier. But it happened. America was at last on its way to growing up.

After the depression of the thirties, America learned a new kind of sacrifice in the first half of the forties; voluntary sacrifice, born of the common goal of survival.

In 1944, volunteers hawked war bonds and planted victory gardens. Twenty million of these were planted, providing one-third of the country's fresh vegetables that year. Between hoeing and harvesting, they collected scrap rubble, scrap metal, and cooking grease. Posters actually asked women to "take your fat cans to the butchers." Since 1943, pleasure driving on the East Coast was banned, and food rationing was imposed nationwide. War production grabbed raw materials, creating shortages that ranged from washing machines and bobby pins to lawn mowers and lobster forks – to a delay of available TV sets.

1944 was not the best of times. But it was a time of awakening. America would never again be the same. And the future would see changes at a far greater pace than ever before in the history of the planet.

This was one hell of a generation you were a part of. Congratulations for having survived it!

In the forties, the dollar was still almighty.

In 1944, the United States spent 95 cents of every government dollar on the war, and the yearly cost of war amounted to $91 billion, bringing the total war cost to $244 1/2 billion since July 1, 1940.

But, by June 30, the end of the government's 1944 fiscal year, the national debt had increased by only $64 billion, to a total of only $201 billion. Only? Remember, we were paying for a World War. And that's pocket change compared to how we're spending money today.

The U.S. matched that debt figure of $201 billion in the first 201 days of fiscal year 1995. Today, we're adding about $1 billion in debt every 24 hours.

And the federal debt has gone from that figure in 1944 of $244 1/2 billion to over $4 trillion today.

The debt stood at $1 trillion as recently as 1981, and has quadrupled since. If the present trend continues, plan on adding three more zeroes to the national debt shortly after the turn of the century.

The purpose of the figures discussed above is not simply to make you aware of how screwed up our elected officials in Washington are these days (Ross Perot already did a pretty good job of that in his fireside flip-chart presentations in the '92 elections), but to get you truly to appreciate the sacrifices made by every American back in the middle 1940s, not only those who worked (and, in some cases, lost) their lives, but also those who stayed home.

A National War Labor Board was established in 1942, charged with the peaceful settlement of labor disputes and to keep salaries stable. The Board's policies worked; between January and August, 1944, basic wage rates rose but 1.3 cents an hour. By August, factory workers were earning but $45.85 a week.

Keep in mind that in 1944, $45 was a lot of money. At that rate of pay, what American workers were able to accomplish was mind boggling. In Chicago, which became the nation's center for the manufacture of armaments, industrial employment stood at 931,000 persons. Chicago's steel mills, 40 blast furnaces strong, poured forth steel day and night, operating near 100% capacity and setting one production record after another. Nearly 18-million tons of steel issued from the Chicago steelmaker's plants per year.

The war effort extracted more than labor. Nearly $12 billion in Victory bonds were sold in Illinois during the war. And in every state in the union, payroll deduction plans were popular. In many factories, 10% of the payroll was going into war bonds. One Chicago family invested $10 a week to buy bonds although its income was only $32 a week.

Back then, the dollar was almighty. Write your congressman (or Congresswoman)!

Former housewives became valuable factory workers when World War II broke out. This woman's job was to install oxygen flask racks above the flight decks of C-87 transport planes.

Good work, Rosey!

In the early forties, when the man of the house went off to war, the woman of the house went to work — in places like this Douglass Aircraft Company plant in Long Beach, California. Here, next door to Rosey the Riveter, these women put the finishing touches on transparent bomber noses for fighter and reconnaissance planes. That was the beginning of a trend that is still growing.

Some 60% of America's mothers now hold down jobs, nearly twice as many as there were as recently as the 1960s. And two-thirds of the new workers hired by the turn of the century will be women.

One of the many good signs of this new independence is that the divorce rate that has been on a steady rise for many years has started headed down. In the future, more women will have support raising their families.

Social and economic factors are also keeping the family intact longer than in the old days (back in your youth). Don't worry so much about your granddaughter not being married. It's a national trend. Young people are leaving the nest much later than you did. In the 1940s, the average American female was around 20 when she first married. Today, she's around 25.

If you're over 50, of either sex, you have to welcome unconditionally this dramatic role shift that's occurred in your lifetime. Women today are a vital and growing part of the nation's labor and political force. Although there is still an often unfair gap between men's and women's salaries, most Americans now agree that should not exist.

Your children and grandchildren, of both sexes, today agree that the workplace is a place where equality should, and will, exist. And today's good marriages are partnerships of equals, not ones in which subservient women play second fiddle and housewives to their husbands and their children.

The trend is indeed up. Today, women own and manage 28% of U.S. businesses. In 1993, women held 20.2% of the seats in state legislatures. And 20 women have been, or are, presidents or prime ministers of their countries.

The sad part of it all, as it is in so many of history's significant mistakes, is that it took so long for it to happen. We tend to forget that it took until 1928 for voting rights to be equalized for American men and women. And mighty powers like Finland, Norway, France, and Japan didn't see the light and grant suffrage until 1945.

Give 'em hell, Rosie!

In Tokyo, Roseys also took a man's jobs in factories. The war drained Japan's manpower, too. By 1944, four million women, like the woman here operating the acetylene torch on an aircraft assembly line,were employed in Japanese war industries. Women were also encouraged to step up the production of a very special commodity: offspring. A propaganda drive's goal was the production of three million births annually - half again as many as in peacetime. Free education was promised for families that produced 10 or more children. Prime Minister Katsuko Tojo's wife almost qualified: she gave birth to seven.

Remember the Victory Gardens? *Well, we weren't the only ones doing it. While we were growing tomatoes in town squares, the Japanese were using available soil to plant crops, too. Here, young volunteers plant rice seedlings in Tokyo's Ueno Park. And everybody in Japan pitched in. By 1945, three million school-aged youths had joined the national labor force.*

**This is why
we didn't build
any cars or tractors or lawn mowers
during the war.**

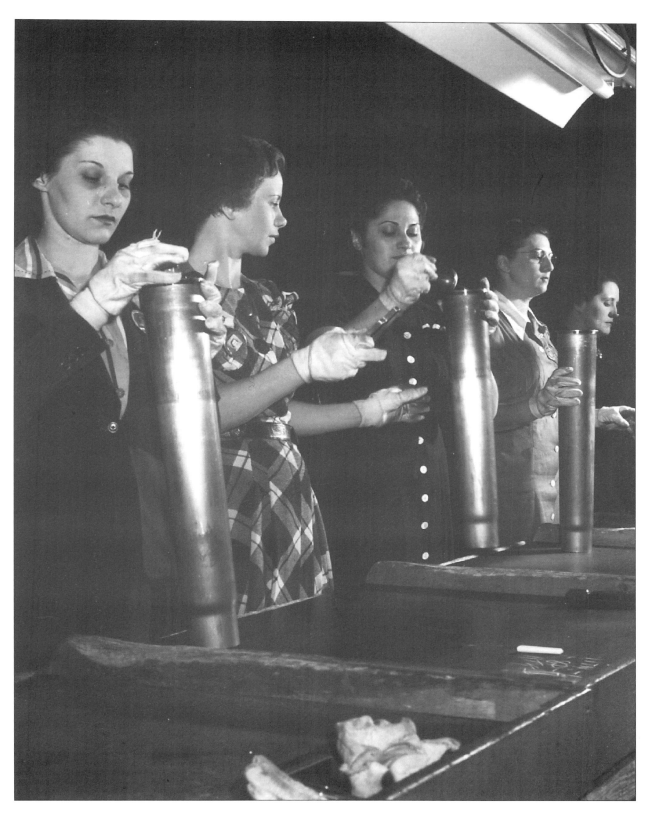

The boys overseas needed ammunition, *and the women back home supplied it.*
These ladies were in charge of final inspection of anti-aircraft cartridges.

**Japanese women
were busy
making bullets, too.**

One of the reasons the Japanese didn't win the war, was because our women
made bigger - and more - bullets.

The Hausfrau also went to work.

By 1941, Germany had seven-million men in military service. As was the case in America and Japan, women had to go to work. They were not as keen on the notion as American and Japanese women, but a massive propaganda effort was launched and the Nazis gave the German Hausfrau little choice. Still, the stubborn ladies were reluctant to leave the hearth. Many went to work, but many stayed home, too. By 1943, three million were slated to go to work in factories. But that number was never reached and, in fact, never rose much above the prewar level.

German men *flew Luftwaffe bombers built by German women.*

When the German men marched off to war, the German women marched off to the fields. *The National Labor Service Program called for women to pull a year's duty doing up to 15-hour stints at slave wages.*

The ladies assembling 88mm shell fuses *in this munitions factory were not happy campers.*

Just how busy were we?

**Between July 1, 1940 and July 31, 1945,
we built**

**296,429 aircraft,
71,062 naval ships,
5,425 cargo ships,
372,431 pieces of artillery,
20,086,061 small arms,
41,585,000,000 rounds of ammunition,
5,822,000 tons of aircraft bombs,
102,351 tanks and self-propelled guns
and 2,455,964 army trucks.**

Before the war, *this lady was one of thousands of housewives in Long Beach, California. When the war broke out, her husband went to war and she went to work.*

Mighty warships of the air, these C-87 planes were built by Consolidated Aircraft
Corporation to transport cargo and troops.

At home,
one of the main
things we sacrificed
was progress.

We learned to make do,
do without
...and wait for things
to get better.

During the depression in the thirties, thousands of farmers left the dust bowl of Arkansas and Oklahoma and headed west to California. This family was one of the few that elected to hold out until things got better. When 1941 rolled around they finally hit the road, realizing that good times were still a long way off.

**Travel was for
those who had
a reason.**

**Civilians stayed
home.**

Gas was rationed, no new cars were being built and trains and busses were reserved for the military. If the trip weren't really necessary, we didn't take it. Most civilians didn't go anywhere until the war was over.

Farm mechanization was something for the future in the forties. Gas was rationed. New trucks and tractors weren't being built. Factories were building planes, tanks and guns. When a machine broke down, it generally stayed broken - or ended up at a recycling center to be turned into planes, tanks and guns.

By planting time in the mid forties, among the people very anxious for the war to end were the thousands of farmers who (A) couldn't get the tractor fixed, (B) didn't have enough ration stamps to get gasoline or (C) didn't yet own a tractor. In the mid forties, most American farmers were in the (C) category.

**Back then, we weren't too picky
about whom we insulted and picked on.**

WASPs were a mean bunch back in the forties. Japanese - Americans weren't the only American citizens to catch their wrath. White folk took it on themselves to discriminate against blacks, reds and browns as well as yellows. Ironically, it won't be too long before America's whites will be in the minority.

This privy was in the Mexican district of San Antonio, Texas in 1940. Back in the forties, outhouses were still widely used. In those days, many Americans ate dinner inside and went to the bathroom outside. After the war, when indoor plumbing became more of a fixture and charcoal grills and patios became popular, the procedure was reversed.

Not everyone was fortunate enough to make big money in war factories. Migrant workers toiled in fields and orchards for as little as 25 cents an hour.

Clothes dryers during the war years were called clothes lines. Most American homes were not yet equipped with such modern appliances as dryers.

Washing clothes wasn't a whole lot of fun, either.

In the forties, the hand saw was a whole lot more popular than the chain saw, mainly because chain saws were scarce and the few there were weighed a ton. To keep the home fires burning, wood cutting in those days was left to men too old and frail to serve and heavy women who didn't have the good fortune to find easier work in factories.

89

Chick Sexing *was crucial to the success of any poultry operation back in the forties. Only the Chick Sexor could tell if a day-old chick were female or worthless cockerel, and a good one (the Chick Sexor) could predict the sex of about 1,000 chicks an hour with 95 percent accuracy. What happened to the cockerels? You don't want to know.*

Would you believe that, back in the forties, they roped horses by hand? Well, you're right. They did. You're a hard person to fool. They still rope horses by hand today. One thing they haven't been able to invent in the past 50 years is an Automatic Stallion Roper Device. It just goes to show that some of those old ways were indeed the best ways. Now don't you feel just a little bit sad about the disappeared Chick Sexor?

Entertainment was a rare diversion in the forties. *On a typical Saturday night, you could count the revelers in Las Vegas on one hand.*

In the forties, there was only one way to pick cotton, and it was not easy. Cotton pickers of that day and age probably wished they'd been born at least 20 years later. This was hard on the back.

When the lumberjacks were called up to active duty, lumberjills went to work. The lady here wielding the pike pole helped other women operate a lumber mill in New Hampshire. In other parts of the country, women took over such jobs as riding logs down rivers, breaking up lumber rafts and falling and trimming trees. It was estimated that for every man in service, five trees had to come down the rivers to build crates in which to send him shelter and equipment. Lumbering became one of the major war industries and one-third of the "man-power" was woman-power.

And here's proof that recycling is not a recent invention.

During the war, everybody collected scrap and turned it into recycling centers. Nothing was refused, from old tires to newspapers to old nylons by the ton.

Hardly anything was burned or thrown out. We recycled rope, twine, gum wrappers, old pillows and clothing. Old nylon was precious. We used it to make parachutes and powder bags for naval guns. And new nylon stockings were put on hold until the war ended.

Nothing went to the junk pile. *This young sailor's old tricycle was turned into bullets.*

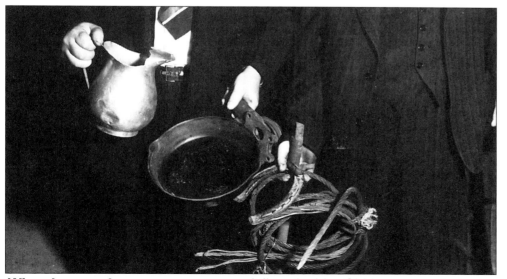

Wire, iron and copper were especially valuable. Old bronze and steel padlocks were worth even more. A bushel basket full of flattened tin cans was also valuable. We even brought bacon grease to the local butcher. He turned it in and it became ammunition.

Recycling was also popular in Japan.

Japanese children gave up their toys. *Anything that was made of plastic or metal was recycled for the war effort.*

Tokyo merchants *collected old bikes and spare parts. And schoolgirls pulled the silver and gold threads out of ceremonial kimonos and turned them in.*

Buddhist monks pitched in. *Here's a group of them turning over precious items from their temple, including their cherished brass gongs. Nothing was spared. Tokyo was stripped of ornamental iron street lamps, railings and brass traffic-line markers. Even the bronze gates to Tokyo's Yasukuni Shrine were dismantled and shipped to a munitions factory. By 1944, military police went from house to house collecting household goods. Each family was allowed only one pot for cooking and one pail for hauling water.*

So was enlisting.

Even sumo wrestlers *signed up. And in Japanese grammar schools, teachers told their students that anybody who did not serve in the "Holy" War would be shamed for life. The propaganda worked. Practically every male in the country old and strong enough to fight answered the call to arms.*

Buddhist monks joined up, too. *The militaristic ardor reached such a peak, the national religion was altered. Until the war, Buddhists believed in non violence. So many Shinto priests enlisted, for the first time in Buddhist history women were ordained to take the men's places.*

Your father's Oldsmobile, the Forties

Oldsmobile started building automobiles in 1897, and continued without interruption until February of 1942, when car production ground to a halt. The Olds slogan became "Keep 'Em Firing," and the company was then engaged in the fulltime production of military items.

Military cannon built by Olds were used on land and in the air. Tank and tank destroyer cannon built by Oldsmobile were of the 75 mm M3 and the 76 mm M1 A1 variety. The company also built the gun tube for the M-10 tank destroyer.

A number of other war-related materials flowed from Oldsmobile's assembly lines. These included crankshafts for English-built Vaxhaul engines used in Army field wagons, tank track end connections, B-26 bomber landing gear cylinders and spiders for the Hamilton three-blade propeller.

During the period from before Pearl Harbor until V-Jay Day, Olds produced 48 million rounds of artillery ammunition, 140,000 aircraft, tank, and other types of cannon, nearly 350,000 precision parts for aircraft engines and over 175 million pounds of forgings for heavy duty trucks, tanks, aircraft, and cannon.

In addition to its military production, Oldsmobile was also used as the location for a series of training classes for Army personnel working with aircraft and tank weapons.

On the human side of the war, a total of 2,255 men left the Lansing, Michigan, Olds plant to enter the armed forces and 52 of those men died in the service.

Like other auto producers, Olds did its best in scrap drives, prompting an interesting battle between factions who wanted to scrap the company's historical auto collections and those who wouldn't hear of such an effort. The savers won out over the scrappers and because of that fact, Oldsmobile today has America's best historical collection of classic cars. Some secretive methods were used like hiding the car collection — which dated back to 1901 — in several obscure posts, including at least one plant roof.

A colorful series of war posters helped motivate the work force. Issues of an eight-page newspaper, and pamphlets entitled "Olds Keeps 'Em Firing" were mailed to all employees.

Your Oldsmobile, the Nineties

You're right; this is not your father's Oldsmobile. Even though Oldsmobile made bullets and cannon 50 years ago, they have made a lot of great cars over the years. But none quite like the new Aurora.

The Aurora is the from the brand new generation of Oldsmobiles. Its clean, smooth shape, with distinctively defined fender bulges and a curving, sweeping roofline, makes it a very unique form for the American road, which is cluttered with thousands of shapes, many of which look very much alike today.

Totally unlike Oldsmobiles from your father's era, there is very little chrome, no grille, and smoothly integrated bumpers. Under this smooth new look is a radically new high-tech platform of rigidity and stiffness. Structural tightness was achieved by extensive computer and scale modeling. The car, though costing much less than other world-class cars such as the Mercedes 300 sedan, equals such cars in stiffness. In fact, it surpasses such expensive imports as Lexus and Infiniti.

The solid foundation supports innovative but proven suspension components. An innovative rack-and-pinion steering mechanism uses an integral rotary electromagnet to smoothly vary the power assist with road speed.

The Aurora engine is not totally new, but it is widely acclaimed. Borrowing from its GM cousin, Cadillac, Olds has developed a smaller bore version of the four-cam 32-valve Northstar V-8, displacing four liters and developing 250 horsepower. A new glass-filled-plastic intake manifold reduces weight and cost, but the engine is otherwise closely related to the 4.6 Cadillac version.

Axle and braking systems are also highly sophisticated, and if you're into that kind of engineering, Oldsmobile guarantees you will be both impressed and satisfied.

Zero to 60 will take you about eight seconds, which is plenty fast enough for anyone but a few teenagers in Modesto, California. Top speed is fast enough to get you arrested in any state in the country. Olds claims the Aurora tops out at 135 mph.

For all this, fuel economy is very good, especially on the highways. Olds figures you should get about 25 mpg on your way to visit the grandkids. And the best part of all is the price: around $32,000.

Bread basket of the World War

During the war years of the forties, over five-million American farmers worked long hours, stretched scarce supplies of machinery and fertilizer and geared their individual operations to state and national goals. War agencies claimed first rights on food production, followed by U.S. citizens and then the Allies and other friendly nations. Armed forces took 25% of the year's food production. Sometimes, for particular foods, the request exceeded the supplies. There was tightening of the food-rationing system, and consumers had to give more points (remember food stamps?) for many rationed items. Every day, the War Food Administration purchased around $8 million worth of food.

In those days, 2 milking machines were called fingers.

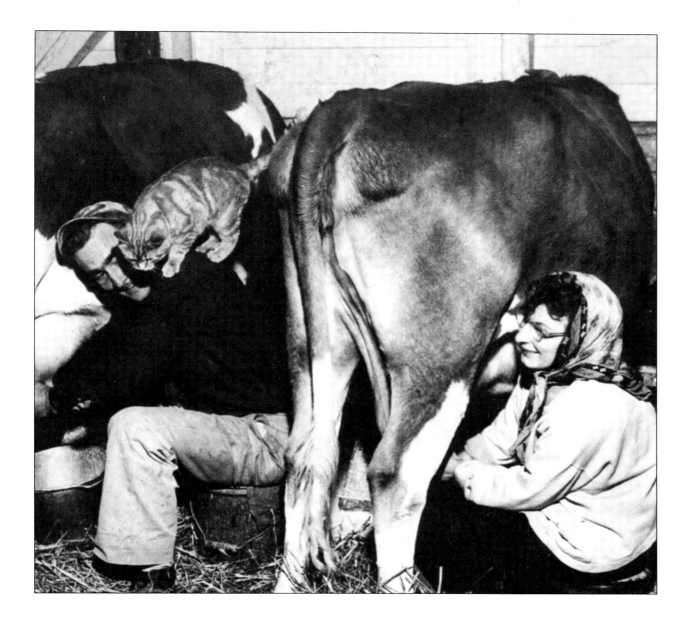

Automatic milking machines didn't come along until after the war. So, like most things in those days, we did it by hand. It did have its good points; it kept the family together. Farm labor was hard to come by during the war, so dairying was still largely a family operation. Hand milking also allowed one to have more personal contact with the cows. But twice a day, 365 days a year? Our dairy farmers did have their hands full.

**Betcha a Coke
you remember the
words to this jingle.**

**Pepsi Cola hits the spot,
Twelve full ounces, that's a lot,
Twice as much for a nickel too,
Pepsi Cola is the drink for you!
Nickel, Nickel. Nickel, Nickel,
Trickle, Trickle, Trickle, Trickle,
Nickel, Nickel. Nickel, Nickel!**

(See...told you that you knew it...you owe us a Coke!)

In the forties, *not everybody had a lot of fun at the beach.*

Marlboro Country wasn't that sexy back in the forties.

Neither were the Marlboro Men.

It has been said that during the forties, every other house on Main Street in Winnemucca, Nevada was a whorehouse. Whether or not that's true will forever be a mystery. Since Winnemucca is stuck out in the middle of nowhere, nobody of reputable reputation ever bothered to check.

Back in the forties, prospecting was a very lonely occupation. It still is. Some things never change.

And some things just disappeared. At one time, the Chicago Union Stock Yards were a mighty city with over a square mile of cattle pens and an immediate neighborhood of 250,000 people. The Yards were still booming in the forties, but now they're long gone.

It was a time for ingenuity and, sometimes, illogical behavior. We had to ration food. And cosmetics and clothing. But our ladies still managed to gussy up. And then it was off to the gas station to wait in line to gas up. Gas, like everything else, was rationed and very hard to come by.

For the first time, we were on our own. The French designers weren't only preoccupied; they were, until 1944, occupied. And not only were we new at this, we also had to make do with a major material shortage. But we were ingenious. If m'lady couldn't afford a new dress, she bought an outrageous hat. And to many of our ladies, the daytime didn't matter; since they were working alongside men, they dressed like men.

The rest of us had no TV to tell us what to do, so we just did what everybody else did — we even dressed like them.

There were no weather reports on the radio — it was supposed to aid the enemy if there were weather forecasts.

So, if it rained on your way to work, your rayon stockings would bag and sag and you were well-advised to put a spare pair in your purse, in case of the unforecast rain.

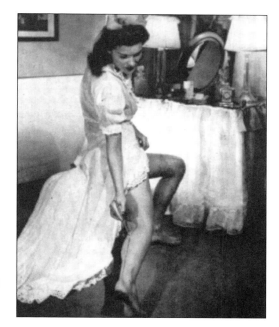

The ladies had to do without silk stockings. *But they had to draw the line somewhere, so they ran it up the back of their legs with an eyebrow pencil, and it did look like a seam.*

If you saw a long line of people, waiting for something, it was a good idea to get in the line yourself.

It was usually for cigarettes, sometimes nylons (but rarely), and sometimes for Scotch. The cigarettes could be any kind — sometimes even chocolate flavored or coffee-flavored tobacco, but cigarettes were hard to come by.

Shoe rationing was two pairs of shoes per year — even for little kids. So even if it wasn't such a good idea, mamas passed shoes along when a child outgrew his.

Meat was rationed, *and a real treat when you could rationalize it. Some foods were even harder to get: butter, peaches and pineapple juice.*

You can tell by the look on their faces that they didn't like what they modeling. But hey, there was a war on. And though it wasn't very attractive, it was fashionable. And, the eagle wings made one feel oh so patriotic.

While France was occupied by the Nazis, fashion in America was nearly paralyzed.

The three-billion dollar U.S. garment industry had always trusted Paris to tell them what styles to create. But with Paris shut off, Americans had to suddenly make those critical decisions themselves.

With typical American ingenuity, we persevered. And our ladies looked magnificent.

Shed a few tears for years gone by. Whatever happened to roller rinks, the Lindy, 78-rpm records, sodas at The Nook, 15-cent burlesque houses, Toni home perms, the BMOC and Rita Hayworth?

111

Fashion in the forties was restricted by more than one factor. Until then, American garment manufacturers had always counted on the French for designs. With France occupied by the Nazis, the Americans had to style clothes themselves. Also, because of material shortages, U.S. Government Regulation L-85 put severe restrictions on such things as depth of hem, number of pockets, and width of belts. Coats were to have no cuffs and no attached hoods or shawls.

In the nineties, all restrictions were off.

In the forties, nonconformity hadn't yet caught on.

It was a great time
to be a milliner.

Ladies who couldn't afford or find stylish dresses could always scrape up the money for something as outrageous as this.

"You make me feel so young." In 1945, Frank Sinatra turned 30 years old.

For the first two-thirds of the decade, as it had been for every decade in our history, there would be no black headliners on center stage in America, with the exception of a few big band leaders. No black singers, actors, comics or sports heroes.

Satchel Paige was still in the Negro Leagues, Lena Horne was playing in Harlem, and when Jackie Robinson left college, he first went to the Negro Leagues.

Meanwhile, white stars Clark Gable, James Stewart, Robert Taylor, Robert Montgomery and John Huston were off at war where they were being entertained by the likes of Ginger Rogers, Fannie Brice, Anne Baxter, Rita Hayworth, Olivia de Haviland, Marlene Dietrich, Katharine Hepburn and Lana Turner.

Soon after the war's end, lots of things would start to change.

It was the era of Swing.

If you're old enough to have listened to the great swing bands of the forties, you heard some truly great bands. But if you're even older and got to hang out in black nightspots in Harlem, N'Orleans, St. Louis and Chicago, you were privileged to hear the best bands in history. And fortunately, many of these black bands were still around when white folks started swingin' over to Swing and white band leaders cashed in on its exploding popularity.

Benny Goodman has gone down in history as the King of Swing. But that's largely because Goodman was white, and the music historians were white. Truth be known, there were a whole bunch of superior musicians and composers before and during Goodman's time who were not white. They even called one of them King: Nat "King" Cole.

Before Cole, way back in 1928 there was a master composer at work perfecting a style and sound that would one day be known as Swing. It took him three years and his residence was Harlem's Cotton Club. Then, in 1932, the 14 instrumentalists and soloist who made up the Duke Ellington band hit the road. The band stayed on it for the next 42 years, doing one-night stands from Hoboken to Hollywood to London and Paris. It became a miracle of physical endurance but it was also rewarded by both artistic and financial success. The Duke played for real kings and hobnobbed with the world's swellest folks for the rest of his life.

Benny Goodman, *the white folks' king of swing*

Ellington's trombone section alone was worth the price of admission. It featured Lawrence Brown, who was extraordinarily versatile. His solo style was unique; it was inimitable. The second member of Ellington's trombone trio was Joe "Tricky Sam" Nanton, whose improvising abilities were also legendary. He's the one who invented "wah wah" and "talking" with the trombone, using a small bathroom plunger over a small mute insert. Nanton's "jungle" style often dominated Ellington's trombone section. The third trombonist was Puerto Rican Juan Trizol, who came from a classical Italian-style band tradition. And these three totally different trombonists were but one-fifth of the Ellington band.

The vocalist in the Ellington organization was Ivie Anderson. Off and on, she shared the job with drummer Sonny Greer and trumpeter Cootie Williams, but in the early forties she became Ellington's full-time vocalist. Lead alto saxophonist Otto Hardwick also signed on for a long run and by the forties the band became stabilized with its instrumental choirs - three trumpets, the three trombones, four reeds (saxes and clarinets), a four-man rhythm section and singer Ivie. It was the zenith of Ellington's career. Combined with the Duke's own powerful and rich piano sound, these performers produced such individual timbers that Ellington had almost as many different sonorities at his disposal as a 90-piece symphony orchestra.

One arrangement that became legendary was *It don't mean a Thing if you ain't got that Swing*. That was first done in 1932, and it was years later before the word Swing became associated in the minds of millions with the "King of Swing," Benny Goodman. During that time, it had been described by jazz musicians like Jelly Roll Morton as a particular rhythmic momentum and feeling. But Ellington beat everybody by a decade in using it in a song title.

And Ellington was so gifted, by the time others took credit for it, Swing was a minor part of his music menu. Blues became so much a part of Ellington's range, there was a long series of songs with that adjective in the title: Blue Harlem, Blue Ramble, Blue Mood, Blue Feelin', Blue Light, Blue Serge and even a bust - Blue Tune. The latter was just too advanced harmonically and too complicated melodically for general public tastes.

As gifted as Ellington was on the piano, there was great competition, including one fellow who could express more ideas into a 32-bar solo than most soloists could manage in an entire evening: Earl Hines. He was 85% blind and had huge hands that could hit keys at amazing velocity. He could double up on double time. Plus, he was always mentally sharp and creative. Nobody ever played Sweet Georgia Brown and Copenhagen better. Throughout his life, Ellington avoided competition with Hines at after-hours sessions.

One of the busiest musicians of the day was the master be-bopper, Dizzy Gillespie

As great as Ellington and Hines were, the musician most responsible for inventing and perfecting swing was Louis Armstrong. He was world famous by the thirties and his followers included Bing Crosby, European intellectuals and hip Americans. He was offered roles in Hollywood musicals, which made him a soloist in society as well as in music.

When it came to Swing, Armstrong was the man. He was a phenomenal horn player. As a musician, he was the one the rest went to school on. And players like Coleman Hawkins, Lester Young, Roy Eldridge and Dizzy Gillespie had a great teacher. And arranger Fletcher Henderson, who was to become Benny Goodman's main arranger years later, was most influenced in his work by Armstrong's rhythmic revolution.

Armstrong goes back, folks. Way back. He was of genius status. People who only remember him as a singer of songs like "Hello Dolly" and "Mack the Knife" were unfortunate. They missed the big show.

In the late twenties, jazz was no more than another rumor about blacks to white America. Hardly any white had heard it in person. Only a handful of whites had actually frequented the black nightspots. And what had been recorded was labeled "race records." Then, in late 1935 and 36, two white

Here's Tommy Dorsey with, you guessed it, the Tommy Dorsey Band

bands became very popular playing hot music in the form of Swing. They were the Casa Loma orchestra and the one headed by Benny Goodman.

Very quickly, other white groups got on the Swing bandwagon. If Benny happened to be booked somewhere else, other options were limitless. The big bands of Artie Shaw, Paul Whiteman, Tommy Dorsey, Bunny Berigan, Xavier Cougat and Harry James roamed the country (Glenn Miller and his orchestra roamed the world until that great director was killed in a plane crash while serving as Director of the U.S.A.F. band). If you missed any of those bands, you could still Swing, and even sway, with Sammy Kaye, Bob Crosby, Xavier Cougat, Orrin Tucker or Kay Kyser.

If those great bands were booked elsewhere, you got a chance to dance to the better bands that had been around for years, the bands of Ellington, Cole, Hines, Dizzy Gillespie, Fletcher or Horace Henderson, Jimmie Lunceford, Chick Webb, Cab Calloway, Fats Waller and Count Basie, to name a few.

By the forties, everybody in the country was into Swing. Places like Chicago's Blackhawk were both booking and broadcasting bands like Goodman's, Miller's and Kyser's as well as featuring stars like Ish Kabibble, Hal Kemp, Jack Teagarden, Jan Garber, Bob Crosby's Bobcats and Les Brown and his Band of Renown.

Mel Torme's career was launched at the Blackhawk, over WGN radio, and Perry Como started there as a singer, at $128 a week.

The hot Swing songs of the forties were great songs. Given a beverage or two to joggle your memory, you can still remember the words to dozens of them.

Below is a list of those golden oldies we all remember from the forties. But we are obliged to give credit where it's due. Louis Armstrong was playing all of them back in 1930 and 1931.

1930

Blue Again *(McHugh)*
Body and Soul *(Green)*
Confessin' *(Dougherty-Reynolds)*
Exactly Like You *(McHugh)*
I Got Rhythm *(Gershwin)*
If I Could Be with You *(James B. Johnson)*
I'm a Ding Dong Daddy *(Baxter)*
Memories of You *(Eubie Blake)*
On the Sunny Side of the Street *(McHugh)*
The Peanut Vendor *(Simons)*
Rockin' Chair *(Carmichael)*
Them There Eyes *(Pinkard)*
You're Lucky to Me *(Eubie Blake)*

1931

Blue Again *(McHugh)*

Body and Soul *(Green)*

Confessin' *(Dougherty-Reynolds)*

Exactly Like You *(McHugh)*

I Got Rhythm *(Gershwin)*

If I Could Be with You *(James B. Johnson)*

I'm a Ding Dong Daddy *(Baxter)*

Memories of You *(Eubie Blake)*

On the Sunny Side of the Street *(McHugh)*

The Peanut Vendor *(Simons)*

Rockin' Chair *(Carmichael)*

Them There Eyes *(Pinkard)*

You're Lucky to Me *(Eubie Blake)*

The Forties: A Great Time For Ol' Broadway!

Carousel

Brigadoon

Kiss Me, Kate

Oklahoma!

South Pacific

Annie Get your Gun

The 20 longest-running
Broadway Shows

(M) denotes musical	**Number of Performances**
1. Chorus Line (M)	6,137
2. Oh! Calcutta! (M)	5,959
3. Cats (M)	4,445
4. 42nd Street (M)	3,486
5. Grease (M)	3,388
6. Fiddler on the Roof (M)	3,242
7. Life with Father	3,224
8. Tobacco Road	3,182
9. Hello, Dolly! (M)	2,884
10. My Fair Lady (M)	2,717
11. Les Miserables (M)	2,534
12. Annie (M)	2,377
13. Man of La Mancha (M)	2,328
14. Abie's Irish Rose	2,327
15. Phantom of the Opera (M)	2,231
16. Oklahoma! (M)	2,212
17. Pippin	1,944
18. South Pacific (M)	1,925
19. Magic Show	1,920
20. Deathtrap	1,792

Radio 1945.

It was a time when the shows were named after the stars, and you got to know them very well, even though you hardly ever, if ever, saw them.

In those days, you sat there looking at the radio. Or, you huddled around it, staring off into space. The kids of today may think that was odd, but nobody ever laughed louder or got more tense. If you don't remember hearing blow-by-blow accounts of Joe Louis championship fights or the knuckle-biting drama of world series games or the hilarity of Jack Benny or Fibber McGee and Molly shows, then you have amnesia. See a doctor.

It was an era the kids will never fully understand. In many homes, folks sat there in the dark or next to kerosene lamps. But nobody left to go outside to the outhouse until the fight or show was over.

For two and a half years there, in the early forties, the top show in broadcasting starred a wooden dummy with a monocle. He was none other than Charlie McCarthy, 38 inches high and all of 40 pounds. His sidekick was Edgar Bergen (yes, kids, this was Candice's dad).

Eleanor Roosevelt *addressed the Democratic National Convention.*

Sunday nights were set aside for an ex-violinist named Jack, and it lasted from 1932 until 1955. Beginning in 1950, he also took on the new thing called television. And by the mid fifties, Jack Benny was a national icon. They also said that his television years never measured up to his radio years.

Remember Bob and Ray? Critics say that they were the freshest thing to hit radio after World War II. In 1940, Minnie Pearl joined the likes of Roy Acuff, Ernest Tubb, and Hank Williams (Senior), PeeWee King and Eddie Arnold on the Grand Ole Opry, and the Opry was one of the most successful programs in radio history.

The Greatest!

Gracie Allen and George Burns met in vaudeville in 1922, and 10 years later had their own radio show. They were an instant hit. One of their ongoing stunts attracted particular attention. On the show, and on others, Gracie conducted a search for her imaginary lost brother. National consternation was such that her real brother had to go into hiding. This may seem like ancient history to some, but it isn't. This is the same George Burns that was still going strong in 1995.

It was a time when big bands like Benny Goodman's and Glenn Miller's were broadcast live from Chicago's Blackhawk Restaurant. Red Barber was the dean of the nation's sportscasters. We heard the news from H.V. Kaltenborn, the "suave voice of doom." And who will ever forget the very popular "Tom Mix and his Straight Shooters" pictured above). Yes, it was great. Those were the Golden Years of radio, my friend.

As the Republican nominee for president, *Wendall L. Willke had radio covering almost all aspects of the election campaign.*

129

You're right. There wasn't any.

"Grandma, you used to dance to *that*?"

Hit songs for 1944

1. Don't Fence Me In
2. Acc-cent-tchu-ate the Positive
3. I Should Care
4. I'll Walk Alone
5. Irresistible You
6. Long Ago and Far Away
7. Put the Blame on Mame
8. Spring will be a Little Late this Year
9. Dream

They made some excellent movies
back in the forties.

The list included *Going My Way,* starring Bing Crosby and Barry Fitzgerald. This won the 1944 Academy Award and Leo McCarey won best director for directing it while Bing won best actor.

Besides Crosby, other top box-office stars of the decade included Bob Hope, Gary Cooper, Betty Grable, Spencer Tracy, Green Garson, Humphrey Bogart, Abbott and Costello, Cary Grant and Bette Davis.

Stars for tomorrow included Sonny Tufts, James Craig, Gloria DeHaven, Roddy McDowell, June Allyson, Barry Fitzgerald, Natalie Wood and Sydney Greenstreet.

Other wonderful movies made in 1944 included *Gaslight* (Charles Boyer and Ingrid Bergman), *The Purple Heart* (Dana Andrews, Richard Loo and Richard Conte), *Lifeboat* (Tallulah Bankhead, Walter Slezak and John Hodiak), *Meet Me in St. Louis* (Judy Garland and Margaret O'Brien, who won a special Oscar for outstanding child actress) and *Cover Girl* (Rita Hayworth and Gene Kelly).

Remember *I Remember Mama?* That was made in 1948. *State Fair* came out in '45, *The Postman Always Rings Twice* and *Anna* and the *King of Siam* in '46. *The Miracle on 34th Street* has been playing since 1947, and in 1948, John Wayne and Montgomery Clift made *Red River.*

In 1948, back from the *Battle of the Bulge,* Marlene Dietrich co-starred with Jean Arthur in *A Foreign Affair* (pictured below).

And if you stayed home,
you could always watch the radio.

To catch the latest gossip, *folks listened to Hedda Hopper.*

Here's the top 10 radio shows *(plus Jack)* for 1944.

1. **Bob Hope**
2. **Fibber McGee and Molly**
3. **Bing Crosby**
4. **Edgar Bergen and Charlie McCarthy**
5. **Joan Davis/Jack Haley**
6. **Walter Winchell**
7. **Radio Theatre**
8. **Abbott and Costello**
9. **Mr. District Attorney**
10. **Eddie Cantor**
11. **Jack Benny**

Sneak Preview: *Rumblings around Hollywood in 1944 had to do with this new picture MGM had in the works. To be called "National Velvet," it would star Reginald Owen with two child actors, Elizabeth Taylor and Mickey Rooney. The picture was released in 1945, and as you well know, became a classic.*

135

Joan Carroll, Judy Garland, Margaret O'Brien and Lucille Bremer, right? *Yes. But can you name the picture? It was a musical, an MGM production, directed by Vincente Minnelli. Got it? "Meet Me in St. Louis?" Right!*

Where's the rest of Orson Wells? *You may have forgotten, but early in his career, Mr. Wells was a very handsome leading man. He was also of normal size. Here he is with Joan Fontaine in the 1944 film "Jane Eyre."*

And here's more of the "Jane Eyre" cast. *Besides Orson Wells and Joan Fontaine, this 1944 movie, directed by Robert Stevenson and co-written by John Houseman, starred Peggy Ann Garner (on the stool), Henry Daniell (pointing), John Sutton, Agnes Moorhead and Margaret O'Brien (in 1944, Margaret was a very busy little girl).*

Barbara Stanwyck, Tom Powers and Fred MacMurray *starred in Paramount's 1944 production of "Double Indemnity," with screenplay by Billy Wilder and Raymond Chandler. The film was directed by Billy Wilder.*

Also playing *in this 1944 blockbuster was Edward G. Robinson.*

138

By 1948, John Ford had discovered both John Wayne and Monument Valley. These were the two most important characters in his 1948 masterpiece, "Fort Apache." In this scene, Wayne (playing Captain York) meets with the Apaches to negotiate a truce.

"Mark Twain" was Fredric March in this Warner Bros. biography of the famous author. And it's a good thing he was, because March's brilliant performance is what saved this otherwise forgettable film. March, who had been a successful film star in the thirties, spent the forties being a success in both stage and film roles.

Vincent Price, Dana Andrews and Gene Tierney *starred in the 1944 film "Laura"...*

...as did Clifton Webb, *who took a bath in it.*

"And the envelope, please..."

With those familiar words, Gary Cooper preceded the announcement of the Oscar for Best Actor for 1944. He handed that prize, as you know, to the gent in the collar at the piano below, Bing Crosby.

The movie itself, *Going My Way,* also got an Oscar, for Best Picture. Its director, Leo McCarey, got another one and Barry Fitzgerald got yet another for Best Supporting Actor. Johnny Burke and Jimmy Van Heusen picked up two more for writing the song "Swinging on a Star." Crosby also sang their title song and "The Day after Forever," as well as the classic Irish ballad, "Too-ra-loo-ra-loo-ra."

Since the popularity of the VCR, this has become a favorite rental film of all ages – especially at Christmas time.

- **The only sisters** to win Oscars did so in the forties. Unless you're really up on movie trivia, this one's tough. Joan Fontaine won one in 1941 and sis Olivia de Haviland got one in 1946 and again in 1949. How come the different last names? Hey, it's Hollywood!

- **The only Oscar to ever win an Oscar?** Actually, he won two, for best song in 1941 and 1945. Give up? It was Oscar Hammerstein the second.

- **Which family can boast of three generations winning Oscars?**
  The Hustons, of course. Grandpa Walter got one for best supporting actor in *The Treasure of the Sierra Madre* in 1948 while papa John got one for directing that film. Daughter Anjelica was 1985's best supporting actress in 1985's *Prizzi's Honor.*

- **Two Oscars for the same performance** went to Harold Russell in 1946. He won Best Supporting Actor and also received an honorary Oscar for his performance in *The Best Years of Our Lives.*

1944's two best actors, *Barry Fitzgerald and Bing Crosby, try to con each other in this scene from the year's best movie: "Going My Way."*

- **The very first non-American film to win** the Oscar for best film of the year was *Hamlet*, in 1948. It was financed and produced in the U.K., and was produced and directed by Sir Laurence Olivier. He also starred in it, achieving the distinction of the only person to ever direct himself to an Oscar. Actually, he was the second to do that. In 1946, Sir Laurence received a special Oscar "for his outstanding achievement as actor, producer and director in bringing *Henry V* to the screen." That film should have won best picture in 1946, but it took two more years for the Hollywood isolationists to recognize greatness from foreign soil.

- **The first director nominated in her or his directing debut** was Orson Welles in 1941, for *Citizen Kane*. And whoever said there aren't any male chauvinists in Hollywood? There has been only one woman nominated for best director: Lina Wertmuller for *Seven Beauties* in 1976. Mr. Welles was also nominated for best actor for his performance in Citizen Kane. That was also his acting debut. He didn't win that, either. He was also up for best producer; didn't win that, either. He did manage to get half an Oscar, for co-writing the film.

- **By 1941, John Ford had won three Oscars.** He was chosen best director for *The Informer* in 1935, *The Grapes of Wrath* in 1940 and *How Green Was My Valley* in 1941. He got a fourth best-director Oscar with *The Quiet Man* in 1952.

- **The only consecutive double-Oscar winner?** That would be Joseph A. Mankiewicz, who won Oscars for best directing and screenplay for *A Letter to Three Wives* in 1949 and *All About Eve* in 1950.

- **It was 1942,** and the little lady was up for her fifth consecutive Oscar. It was ...Bette

142

Davis. All told, she was nominated for best actress 10 times and won twice. That puts her in second place. Katharine Hepburn was nominated for best actress 12 times and won four times.

- **Montgomery Clift** made his acting debut in 1948. He did so well in *The Search,* he was nominated for best actor. Did he win an Oscar? No. Sorry, Montgomery.

- **In 1944,** Barry Fitzgerald was up for two Oscars, for best actor and for best supporting actor in *Going My Way.* He lost the best-actor prize to co-star Bing Crosby. But he still ended up with two Oscars. He lopped the head off his best-supporting-actor Oscar while practicing his golf swing and Paramount gave him a replacement.

Bing Crosby and Barry Fitzgerald *play out another scene from the Oscar winner, "Going My Way."*

- **After being nominated three times for Oscars in the thirties,** Greta Garbo was shut out in the forties. She finally won an honorary Oscar in 1954, but sent someone else to collect it.

- **When Bing Crosby beat out co-star Barry Fitzgerald** for the best-actor Oscar in 1944, Bing very nearly missed the show. He was playing golf that day and Paramount officials had to drag him off the course to head downtown for the awards ceremony. Bing was astonished when he won.

- **The most embarrassed lady** in Hollywood on Oscar night in 1947 had to be Rosalind Russell. So sure was she that she was going to win the Oscar for best actress (for her performance in *Mourning Becomes Electra*), she stood up to accept the award before the envelope was opened. An early edition of the *Los Angeles Times* had declared Rosalind the winner. But the award went instead to Loretta Young, for her performance in *The Farmer's Daughter.* Ironically, Rosalind had been offered that role, but turned it down for the *Mourning* role.

143

The 5 most beautiful women you ever saw.

Elizabeth Taylor

Marilyn Monroe

Lena Horne

Sophia Loren

Grace Kelly

The greatest movies of all time?

When it comes to great movies, don't let the kids kid you. They may know plenty about what's hot, but you can tell them something about what's great.

Movies, unlike television, aren't a recent invention.

In fact, it was back before the turn of this century, in 1896, when a very popular stage comedienne named May Irwin teamed with an actor named John C. Rice to repeat a scene from their stage success, *The Widow Jones,* for the experimental cameras of a fellow named Thomas Alva Edison. It was a very brief scene (fifty feet of film), involving Miss Irwin and the mustachioed Rice in a rather prolonged kiss. To the shock and dismay of many, including members of the clergy, the couple seemed to be enjoying their on-camera smooch. One indignant writer proclaimed it close to "indecent in its emphasized vulgarity, a lyric of the Stock Yards," and called for police interference.

The movie version was called *The Kiss,* and needless to say, this scandalous short became an instant sensation, and the earliest indication that the subject of romance would clearly flourish on the screen.

And that was half a century before you were born!

Lots of great movies were made before, and during, your lifetime. But, in our opinion, it's the ones before that stand out. To test our theory, try this: Think of around 20 or 30 of the old timers — from Chaplin to Bogart. Now try to think of 20 or 30 of the new stars. It's a lot harder, isn't it?

True, they don't make movies like they used to. A lot of people think they don't make them as well. This is certainly a debabatable subject, but in 1987, 80 top film people from around the world sat down and put together their all-time greats.

That list is on the facing page. You may argue with it if you wish, but don't write us. Write the film makers; it's their list.

SOURCE: From *JOHN KOBAL PRESENTS THE TOP 100 MOVIES* by John Kobal. Copyright by John Kobal and the The Kobal Collection. Used by permission of New American Library, a division of Penguin Books USA Inc.

Here's the list.

1. *Citizen Kane*/Orson Welles (U.S. 1940)

2. *The Rules of the Game*/Jean Renoir (France, 1939)

3. *Battleship Potemkin*/Sergei Eisenstein (USSR, 1925)

4. *8 1/2*/Frederico Fellini (Italy, 1963)

5. *Singin' in the Rain*/Gene Kelly & Stanley Donen (U.S., 1952)

6. *Modern Times*/Charles Chaplin (U.S., 1935)

7. *Wild Strawberries*/Ingmar Bergman (Sweden, 1957)

8. *The Gold Rush*/Charles Chaplin (U.S., 1925)

9. *Casablanca*/Michael Curtiz (U.S., 1942)

10. *Rashomon*/Akira Kurosawa (Japan, 1950)

11. *The Bicycle Thief*/Vittorio De Sica (Italy, 1948)

12. *City Lights*/Charles Chaplin (U.S., 1931)

13. *Children of Paradise*/Marcel Carne (France), 1945)

14. *Sunrise*/F.W. Murnau (U.S., 1927)

15. *The Earrings of Madame De ... a.k.a. Diamond Earrings*/Max Ophuls (France/Italy, 1953)

16. *Grand Illusion*/Jean Renoir (France/Italy, 1953)

17. *The Searchers*/John Ford (U.S., 1956)

18. *2001: A Space Odyssey*/Stanley Kubrick (Great Britain, 1968)

19. *Some Like it Hot*/Billy Wilder (U.S., 1959)

20. *Ivan the Terrible,* Parts I & II/Sergei Eisenstein (USSR,1941-1945)

21. *Jules and Jim*/Francois Truffault (France, 1961)

22. *Stagecoach*/John Ford (U.S., 1939 – pictured above)

23. *Vertigo*/Alfred Hitchcock (U.S., 1958)

24. *The Seven Sumarai*/Akira Kurosawa (Japan, 1954)

25. *Tokyo Story*/Yasujiro Ozu (Japan, 1953)

In 1940, Orson Wells released his first film. *He was the producer, co-writer and star of one of the greatest movies ever made. Mr. Welles was 25 years old when he made "Citizen Kane."*

So much for the film makers' opinion; here are the 20 highest -grossing films of all time.

(adjusted for inflation)

1.	Gone with the Wind (1939)	$805,856,000
2.	Snow White and the Seven Dwarfs (1937)	$606,525,700
3.	Star Wars (1977)	$450,912,400
5.	The Sound of Music (1965)	$357,428,400
6.	Jaws (1975)	$339,419,500
7.	101 Dalmatians (1961)	$323,583,600
8.	The Godfather (1972)	$290,804,100
9.	The Exorcist (1973)	$282,409,000
10.	The Jungle Book (1967)	$257,478,000
11.	The Sting (1973)	$248,177,200
12.	The Empire Strikes Back (1980)	$242,244,400
13.	Return of the Jedi (1983)	$239,139,400
14.	Grease (1978)	$208,252,700
15.	Close Encounters of the Third Kind (1977)	$192,556,400
16.	Ghostbusters (1984)	$182,228,700
17.	Raiders of the Lost Ark (1981)	$179,295,500
19.	Love Story (1970)	$176,854,400
20.	American Graffiti (1973)	$174,930,100

Two views of Jane Russell

The noted chauvinist Bob Hope used to introduce Jane Russell this way: "Here comes the two and only Jane Russell."

Back in the forties, shots like these were considered very risque. In her first movie, *The Outlaw,* Ms. Russell wore a low-cut peasant blouse while sucking on a straw in a haystack. This kind of wanton behavior infuriated a lot of people. In Baltimore, a judge upheld a Maryland censorship case against the movie, declaring "Miss Russell's breasts hung over the picture like a thunderstorm over a landscape. They were everywhere."

The controversy's counter from a judge in San Francisco, who handed down an acquittal: "We have seen Jane Russell. She is an attractive specimen of American womanhood. God made her what she is."

Just how much have the censors eased up in 50 years?

Well, back in 1940, after waiting three years for a decision, Howard Hughes exhibited *The Outlaw* without a Seal of Approval. This was the first serious breach of the Production Code since its inception in 1934.

The next serious breach occurred in 1954, when Otto Preminger distributed *The Moon is Blue,* a comedy about virginity, without a Seal of Approval. Just how risque was *The Outlaw?* Well, if you remember it, you'll consider it pretty tame when compared to what you and the kids are watching today, even on TV.

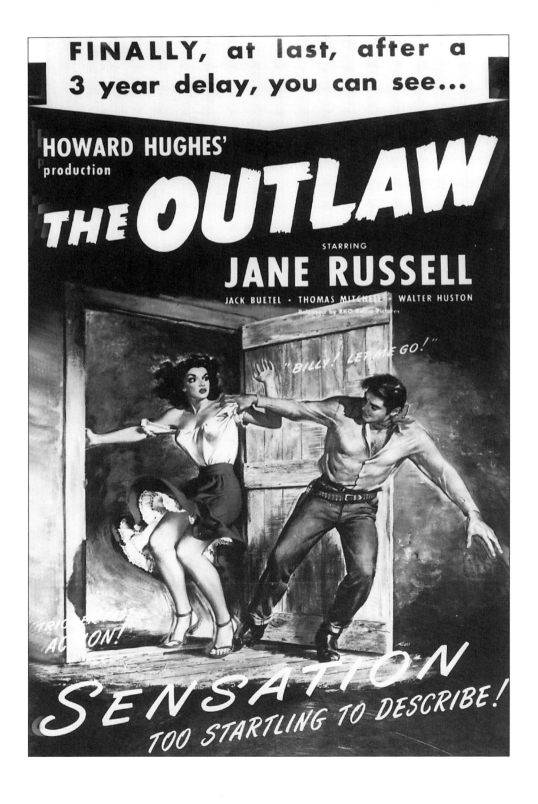

Whatever did they do
before they became famous?

Dana Andrews was an accountant.

Humphrey Bogart was in the navy.

Ernest Borgnine drove a truck. He hauled vegetables.

Clara Bow was a receptionist in a doctor's office.

Peter Boyle was a monk.

Charles Bronson was a coal miner in Pennsylvania.

Joe E. Brown played pro football in St. Paul.

James Caan was a rodeo rider.

Rory Calhoun was a boxer.

Maurice Chevalier was an electrician.

Gary Cooper sold magazine ad space.

Joan Crawford did laundry.

Nelson Eddy was a switchboard operator.

Douglas Fairbanks manufactured soap.

Clark Gabel was a telephone repairman.

Greta Garbo was an assistant in a barber shop.

Sterling Hayden was a sea captain.

Andy Griffith was a high school music teacher.

Rock Hudson was a postman.

Sir Alec Guinness was an advertising copywriter.

John Huston was a Mexican cavalry officer.

Deborah Kerr was a British heiress.

Jack Palance was a boxer.

Raquel Welch was a cocktail waitress.

Sylvester Stallone cleaned lion cages.

Whatever happened
to Big Little Books?

They went out of print many years ago.

Hopefully, you saved yours.

They used to cost a nickel.

This one cost $30 at a book fair in Evanston, Illinois in 1994.

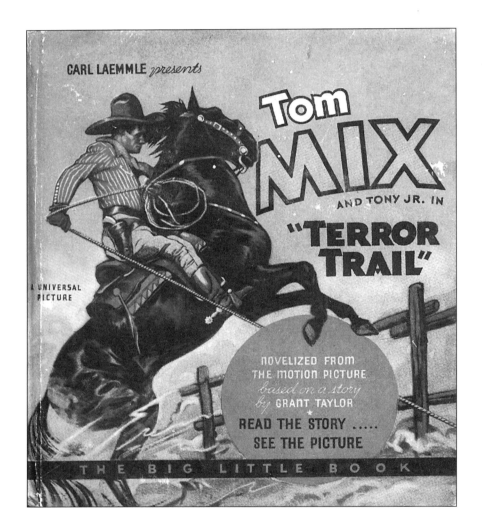

Surely you've already guessed, but in case you need proof for the kids, that's Jack Benny on the left and Milton Berle on the right. Jack is supposed to be Ben Hur and Milton is Cleopatra. Drag was a favorite costume of Uncle Miltie's. The famed comedian was host of television's hottest show, the Texaco Star Theater, from 1948 until 1956 (he was so popular, they renamed it the Milton Berle Show in 1953). In the final two episodes of his show, Berle introduced the world to a future star - a young singer by the name of Elvis Presley.

By the end of the decade,
Jack, Uncle Miltie, Kukla, Fran and Ollie
were household names.

When the decade started, barely a handful of TV sets existed. RCA inaugurated scheduled telecasting at the 1939 New York World's Fair, with just a few TVs available for sale. But the anticipated boom quickly stopped. World War II interrupted the development of the television industry, with most electronics research being devoted to war production. Television stayed on hold until after the war; then production renewed. Milton Berle was the first network star. He was the host of the *Texaco Star Theater* on the NBC radio network, but it was his role in that show on the tube that made him a household name in the late forties. By the time 1948 rolled around, television was well on its way. On Tuesday nights, when Berle's show went on the air, streets emptied as people flocked to nightspots and living rooms of the neighbors. Some families even put their tubes in their front windows so the whole block could enjoy the show.

By 1950, one million affluent Americans owned TV sets. In this ad photo for RCA, a family enjoys Kukla, Fran and Ollie.

Big Games Without the Big Names

For four long years, they played the big games without the big names.

By the middle of the forties, mediocrity hit the bright lights of pro sports. With the main baseball talent off at war and a galaxy of goofballs trying to fill their shoes, the public turned to the then next-best thing. For the first time, college football became the nation's number one sport.

1941-45: When the goofballs got to play major league baseball. *This sad assortment of over-the-hillers and bewildered misfits is somewhat typical of major league teams in the war years of the forties. This particular group was known as Philadelphia's "Phutile" Phillies.*

The greatest hitter
who never played...

...in the very prime of his life, was Ted Williams. This raw-boned kid came to Boston from San Diego in 1939, all six foot three and 160 pounds of him, and hit .327, blasted 31 home runs

Ted Williams, the greatest hitter the game has ever known, shown here in the early forties shaking hands with the game's king of swat, Babe Ruth.

and knocked in 145 runners to lead the American League. By 1941, he was even better. While rival Joe DiMaggio was grabbing headlines with a 56-game hitting streak, Williams out-hit DiMaggio during the streak, .412 to .408. Williams finished that season with 185 hits in 456 at-bats, for a .406 average. In the All Star game that year, Williams came to bat with two on and two out. He hit a home run and the American League won, 7 to 5.

In 1942, Williams went off to the war to fly fighter planes. When he came back, he won four American League home run titles. He also won the triple crown in 1947, to equal his 1942 feat. He led the league in slugging percentage nine times.

His baseball career was interrupted again when he was called back into service to fly combat with the Marines in Korea. In this war, the great hitter was hit by ground fire but still managed to land his badly charred plane. But he was far from through with baseball. In 1957, Williams led the league with .388 and he also hit 38 home runs. The next year, he again led the league with a .328 average. And in 1960, at age 42, Ted Williams bid farewell to baseball by hitting 29 homers, including, appropriately, one in his final game.

The greatest hitter of all time accomplished the distinction by sitting out five full seasons due to military service and two major injuries.

In 1942, major leaguers Joe Coleman, Johnny Sain, Ted Williams, Johnny Pesky and Buddy Gremp traded baseball uniforms for flight suits.

Baseball got so bad during the war, St. Louis played St. Louis in the 1944 World Series. Then the war ended and the stars came back for the game's finest hour.

The Yankees won the pennant 13 times, the Giants were still playing in the Polo Grounds, and the player who roamed that outfield was "Say Hey" Willie Mays. If you got to watch baseball in the 40s and 50s, you were privileged to see the game at the best it ever was. And it will never be that good again.

Joe DiMaggio was almost as good of a hitter as Ted Williams. He was so smooth he made the game look incredibly easy. He never made mistakes. Not rarely. Never. And he was a winner. When he arrived in New York in 1936, the Yankees hadn't been in the World Series since 1932. They were in six of the next seven. Like Williams, DiMaggio was off to the war in the prime of his career. But his 361 career home runs and 1,537 runs batted in are even more remarkable when you consider the three years he lost to the service. His 56-game hitting streak in 1941 is one of baseball's most amazing feats.

AMERICAN LEAGUE:

1B	Mickey Vernon
2B	Joe Gordon
3B	Al Rosen
SS	Lou Boudreau
OF	Ted Williams
OF	Mickey Mantle
OF	Joe DiMaggio
C	Yogi Berra
P	Bob Feller
P	Bob Lemon
UTIL	Minnie Minoso
MGR	Casey Stengel

159

NATIONAL LEAGUE:

1B	Stan Musial
2B	Red Schoendist
3B	Eddie Mathews
SS	Ernie Banks
OF	Willie Mays
OF	Duke Snider
OF	Ralph Kiner
C	Roy Campanella
P	Robin Roberts
P	Warren Spahn
UTIL	Luke Easter
MGR	Billy Southworth

When they got through fighting and started playing again, 44 of them made it all the way to the Hall of Fame.

Richie Ashburn . . . Outfielder	**Mel Ott** . . . . Outfielder
Lou Boudreau . . . . . Shortstop	**Satchel Paige** . . . . . Pitcher
Roy Campanella . . Catcher	**Pee Wee Reese** . . . Shortstop
Joe Cronin . . . . Shortstop	**Phil Rizzuto** . . . . . . Shortstop
Dizzy Dean . . . . Pitcher	**Robin Roberts** . . . . Pitcher
Bill Dickey . . . . Catcher	**Jackie Robinson** . . Second Base
Joe DiMaggio . . . . . Outfielder	**Red Ruffing** . . . . . . Pitcher
Bobby Doerr . . . . . Second Base	**Red Schoendist** . . . Second Base
Bob Feller . . . . Pitcher	**Enos Slaughter** . . . Outfielder
Rick Ferrell . . . . . . Catcher	**Duke Snider** . . . . . . Outfielder
Jimmie Foxx . . . . . First Base	**Warren Spahn** . . . . Pitcher
Hank Greenberg . . First Base	**Arky Vaughn** . . . . . Shortstop
Billy Herman . . . . . Second Base	**Lloyd Waner** . . . . . . Outfielder
Monte Irvin . . . . Outfielder	**Paul Waner** . . . . . . Outfielder
George Kell . . . . . . Third Base	**Ted Williams** . . . . . . Outfielder
Ralph Kiner . . . . . . Outfielder	**Early Wynn** . . . . Pitcher
Ernie Lombardi . . . Catcher	**Leo Durocher** . . . . . Manager
Bob Lemon . . . . . . Pitcher	**Bucky Harris** . . . . . Manager
Ted Lyons . . . . Pitcher	**Connie Mack** . . . . . Manager
Joe Medwick . . . . . Outfielder	**Joe McCarthy** . . . . Manager
Johnny Mize . . . . . . First Base	**Bill McKechnie** . . . . Manager
Stan Musial . . . . . . Outfielder, First Base	**Casey Stengel** . . . . Manager
Hal Newhouser . . . . Pitcher	

All of the players and managers listed above were in the major leagues between 1945 and 1950.

The MVPs of the Big Leagues in the forties

National League:

1940	◊ Frank McCormick Cin		1st Base	19 HR	127 RBI	191 Hits*	.309 Av.	
1941	◊ Dolph Camilli	Bklyn	1st Base	34 HR*	120 RBI*	.285 Av.		
1942	◊ Mort Cooper	StL	Pitcher	22 Wins*	7 Losses	1.78 ERA*	10 SO*	
1943	◊ Stan Musial	StL	Outfield	13 HR	81 RBI	220 Hits*	.357 Av.*	
1944	◊ Marty Marion	StL	Shortstop	F.A.	.972*	63 RBI		
1945	◊ Phil Cavaretta	Chi	1st Base	6 HR	97 RBI	.355 Av.*		
1946	◊ Stan Musial	StL	1st B,OF	103 RBI	124 Runs*	228 Hits*	.365 Av.*	
1947	Bob Elliott	Bos	3rd Base	22 HR	113 RBI	.317 Av.		
1948	Stan Musial	StL	OF	39 HR	131 RBI*	.376 Av.*		
1949	◊ Jackie Robinson	Bklyn	2nd Base	16 HR	124 RBI	37 SB*	.342 Av.*	

American League:

1940	◊ Hank Greenberg	Det.	OF	41 HR*	150 RBI*	50 2B*	.340 Av.	
1941	◊ Joe DiMaggio	NY	OF	30 HR	125 RBI*	.357 Av.		
1942	◊ Joe Gordon	NY	2nd Base	18 HR	103 RBI	.322 Av.		
1943	◊ Spud Chandler	NY	Pitcher	20 Wins*	4 Losses	1.64 ERA*	5 SO**	
1944	Hal Newhouser	Det.	Pitcher	29 Wins*	9 Losses	2.22 ERA*	187 K*	
1945	◊ Hal Newhouser	Det.	Pitcher	25 Wins*	9 Losses	1.81 ERA*	8 SO*	212 K*
1946	◊ Ted Williams	Bos	OF	38 HR	123 RBI	142 Runs*	.342 Av.	
1947	◊ Joe DiMaggio	NY	OF	20 HR	97 RBI	.355 Av.		
1948	◊ Lou Boudreau	Clev	Shortstop	18 HR	106 RBI	.355 Av.		
1949	◊ Ted Williams	Bos	OF	43 HR*	159 RBI**	150 Runs*	.343 Av.	

◊ Played for pennant winner. * Led League. **Tied for league lead.

Like Babe Ruth, Stan Musial *started out as a pitcher. Then he learned how to swing the bat, and for 13 straight seasons he had at least 183 hits. He didn't hit 'em as far as Ruth, but he did know how to connect. His career doubles mark (725) was beaten only by Tris Speker and Pete Rose. Only Hank Aaron had more extra-base hits. Musial won the MVP award three times in the forties and also led the St. Louis Cardinals to the World Series three times. With a year out for the military in 1945, he played 22 seasons with the St. Louis Cardinals and finished his illustrious career with a lifetime batting average of .331.*

In the 1944 Negro Leagues' East-West All Star game, some stars were missing.

The 1944 World Series, which traditionally featured the best two white teams in the majors, wasn't the only fall classic to fall on hard times. The National Colored All Star Game, featuring the best players from the Negro Leagues, also had its troubles. Played annually those days in Chicago's Comiskey Park, this classic annually drew over 50,000 fans. But in 1944, they played the game without many of their stars (50 were off fighting the war). One star who could have played was the legendary Satchel Paige. But Satchel was paid only $100 for his '43 performance, and league owners refused to up the ante for '44.

When Satchel's proposal that proceeds be donated to the war effort was turned down by the owners, Satchel decided to sit that one out.

When Satchel Paige finally got to the major leagues, in 1948, it was at the end of an already brilliant career. Satchel, for one, considered the first part of his career the most glorious part, by far. When congratulated for having a great first season with the Cleveland Indians and told he might well be named Rookie of the Year, the irrepressible Paige replied, "22 years is a long time to be a rookie."

Paige began his career in 1926 with the Chattanogga Black Lookouts. In 1939, Joe DiMaggio stated that Satchel Paige was "unquestionably the greatest pitcher I've ever faced in my life."

NO 498
PRESS
COMISKEY PARK
NATIONAL COLORED ALL STAR
BASEBALL GAME
Sun., Aug. 16, 1942
—3:00 p.m.—
If legal game is not played, this rain check to be refunded. See daily papers for notice and manner of refund.

Just how good were the players in the Negro Leagues? Better than the whites, claim many.

Two of the greatest catchers in baseball history played in the Negro Leagues (Roy Campanella, left, and Josh Gibson, below). Campanella was young enough to play in the majors, but when the color line was broken, Gibson was too old. Both men are today enshrined in the Hall of Fame.

Ted Strong was one of the many extraordinary athletes who performed in the Negro Leagues. Strong played for the Kansas City Monarchs from 1942-46 and also played guard for the basketball Harlem Globetrotters from 1940-47. Umpire Jocko Conlon said of Strong and his contemporaries, "All these colored ballplayers would have been stars in the big leagues today, given the chance."

In 1944, 6'10" George Mikan
was the dominant giant
in college basketball.

George Mikan was a gifted young man who had two distinct advantages over everybody else playing college basketball in 1944.

First, since he'd spent eight years of intense training on the piano, he had the finger strength and dexterity to control the ball on his fingertips much more easily than his peers. Secondly, he was 6'10." And thirdly, his coach was a slave-driving perfectionist named Ray Meyer (yup, same guy who coached DePaul into the late eighties) who got George over his awkwardness by putting him through daily routines of skipping rope, shadowboxing, punch-

ing a bag, sparring, dancing and drills with smaller, quicker players.

Ray also made George shoot 200 right-hand hook shots and 200 left-hand hook shots every day.

The result of all this effort was that George was eventually named The Basketball Player of the First Half of the Twentieth Century.

In 1944, as a sophomore, George was already good enough to be named to the All America team (he led the country in scoring his next two years).

The highlight of DePaul's 1944 season was the NIT semifinals, which matched DePaul with Oklahoma A&M and its 7' Bob Kurland, in the first "Battle of the Giants."

DePaul won, 41-38, but lost to St. Johns in the finals (they won it in '45, and George averaged 40 points a game in that tournament).

And this is how the hottest shooter in the pros launched his long shots.

Bobby McDermott was one of those players who was in the right league at the right time. The shot that gave him a 20-point-per-game average in 1944 wouldn't cut it in high schools gyms today.

This was no fault of Bobby's, mind you. In 1944, even pros were taught that when shooting from the perimeter, they should only do so when they were in their "platform," meaning they should have both feet anchored solidly to the floor. The only way for the 5'11" Bobby to develop thrust to get the ball to the hoop was to start it at waist level and bring it up with both hands: the classic two-handed set shot.

In 1944, the one-handed jump shot was something for the future, although Stanford's Hank Luisetti did perfect it on his way to becoming a national hero way back in 1938. But Hank defected to Hollywood, where he bombed, then to play basketball in the navy, where he came down with spinal meningitis in 1944. He recovered, but lost the chance for a lucrative pro career.

But back to Bobby. To be blunt, pro basketball in 1944 was in a pathetic state. There were but six teams, and two of those were called the Sheboygan Redskins and the OshKosh All-Stars. Bobby played for the Fort Wayne Pistons. A crowd of over 15,000 watched them dismantle the Dayton Acmes 78-52 to win their second straight world tournament.

Bobby led all scorers with 21 points. Blackie Towery, who managed to get a military leave, also got into the record books with a season total of one point.

In 1944, Utah got two chances to win a national championship.

In 1944, Utah was invited to the NCAA basketball tournament, but turned the offer down for the NIT because several of their players had never been to New York. But, the western sightseers lost in that tournament in the first round. When Arkansas had to drop out of the NCAA because of an auto accident that injured several players, Utah got the second chance - and made the most of it.

Arnie Ferrin was Utah's main man for both the season and both tournaments. He was very happy for the second chance. He won the NCAA Tourney MVP trophy to go along with selection to the 1944 All America team.

Close guarding *by Dartmouth kept the score close in the 1944 NCAA finals. So close, the game against Utah went into overtime before Utah finally prevailed, 42-40.*

The Aggies of Oklahoma A&M won the NCAA's basketball tournament in 1945. Notice the lack of blacks on the team? There weren't many playing college basketball back in 1945. Fortunately, that was all about to change.

Basketball's 7-footers, 1944.

1.   Bob Kurland

The NBA's 7-footers, 1994.

1.   Patrick Ewing
2.   Shaquille O'Neal
3.   Benoit Benjamin
4.   Dwayne Schintzius
5.   Matt Geiger
6.   Robert Parish
7.   Kevin Duckworth
8.   Bill Cartwright
9.   Will Perdue
10. Brad Daugherty
11. Rik Smits
12. Olden Polynice
13. Kevin Willis
14. Jan Koncak
15. Hakeem Olajuwan
16. David Robinson
17. Felton Spencer
18. Mark Eaton
19. Dikembe Mutombo
20. Luc Longley
21. Donald Hodge
22. Joe Kleine
23. Rick King
24. Vlade Divac
25. James Edwards
26. Stanley Roberts
27. Elmore Spencer
28. Shawn Bradley

NCAA Final Fours for the forties

1940   Indiana beat Kansas in the finals, 60 to 42...Duquesne beat Southern Cal to finish third. Indiana's coach was Branch McCracken. MVP was Indiana's Marv Huffman.

1941   Wisconsin beat Washington State in the finals, 39 to 34...Pittsburgh beat Arkansas to finish third. Wisconsin's coach was Harold Foster. MVP was Wisconsin's John Kotz.

1942   Stanford beat Dartmouth in the finals, 53 to 38...Colorado beat Kentucky to finish third. Stanford's coach was Everett Dean. MVP was Stanford's Howard Dallmar.

1943   Wyoming beat Georgetown in the finals, 46 to 34...Texas beat DePaul to finish third. Wyoming's coach was Everett Shelton. MVP was Wyoming's Ken Sailors.

1944   Utah beat Dartmouth in overtime in the finals, 42 to 40...Iowa State beat Ohio State to finish third. Utah's coach was Vadal Peterson. MVP was Utah's Arnie Ferrin.

1945   Oklahoma A&M beat NYU in the finals, 49 to 45...Arkansas beat Ohio State to finish third. Oklahoma A&M's coach was Hank Iba. MVP was Oklahoma A&M's Bob Kurland.

1946   Oklahoma A&M beat North Carolina 43 to 40 in the finals...Ohio State beat California to finish third. Oklahoma A&M's coach was Hank Iba. MVP was Oklahoma A&M's Bob Kurland.

1947   Holy Cross beat Oklahoma 58 to 47 in the finals...Texas beat CCNY to finish third. Holy Cross's coach was Alvin Julian. MVP was Holy Cross's George Kaftan.

1948   Kentucky beat Baylor 58 to 42 in the finals...Holy Cross beat Kansas State to finish third. Kentucky's coach was Adolph Rupp. MVP was Kentucky's Alex Groza.

1949   Kentucky beat Oklahoma State 46 to 36 in the finals...Illinois beat Oregon State in the finals. Kentucky's coach was Adolph Rupp. MVP was Kentucky's Alex Groza.

1939-40	The New York Rangers beat the Toronto Maple Leafs in six games.
1940-41	The Boston Bruins beat the Detroit Red Wings in six games.
1941-42	The Toronto Maple Leafs beat the Detroit Red Wings in seven games.
1942-43	The Detroit Red Wings beat the Boston Bruins in four games.
1943-44	The Montreal Canadiens beat the Chicago Blackhawks in four games.
1944-45	The Toronto Maple Leafs beat the Detroit Red Wings in seven games.
1945-46	The Montreal Canadiens beat the Boston Bruins in five games.
1946-47	The Toronto Maple Leafs beat the Montreal Canadiens in six games.
1947-48	The Toronto Maple Leafs beat the Detroit Red Wings in four games.
1948-49	The Toronto Maple Leafs beat the Detroit Red Wings in four games.
1949-50	The Detroit Red Wings beat the New York Rangers in seven games.

...and in the forties, nobody tried to disfigure a figure skater with an iron pipe.

World Figure Skating Champions

Women:

1940-46	No Competition, due to the war, not some crazed assailant.
1947	Barbara Ann Scott, Canada.
1948	Barbara Ann Scott, Canada.
1949	Alena Vrzanova, Czechoslovakia.
1950	Alena Vrzanova, Czechoslovakia.

Pairs:

1940-46	No Competition.
1947	Micheline Lannoy, Pierre Baugniet, Belgium.
1948	Micheline Lannoy, Pierre Baugniet, Belgium.
1949	Andrea Kekessy, Ede Kiraly, Hungary.
1950	Karol Kennedy, Peter Kennedy, United States.

Men:

1940-46	No Competition.
1947	Hans Gerschwiler, Switzerland.
1948	Dick Button, United States.
1949	Dick Button, United States.
1950	Dick Button, United States.

Wimbledon Winners

Women

1940-45 No Tournament.

1946 Pauline Betz beat Louise Brough, 6-2, 6-2.

1947 Margaret Osborne beat Doris Hart, 6-2, 6-4.

1948 Louise Brough beat Doris Hart, 6-3, 8-6.

1949 Louise Brough beat Margaret Osborne duPont, 10-8, 1-6, 10-8.

1950 Louise Brough beat Margaret Osborne duPont, 6-1, 3-6, 6-1.

Men

1940-45 No Tournament.

1946 Yvon Petra beat Geoff E. Brown, 6-2, 6-4, 7-9, 5-7, 6-4.

1947 Jack Kramer beat Tom P. Brown, 6-1, 6-3, 6-2.

1948 Bob Falkenburg beat John Bromwich, 7-5, 0-6, 6-2, 3-6, 7-5.

1949 Ted Schroeder beat Jaroslav Drobny, 3-6, 6-0, 6-3, 4-6, 6-4.

1950 Budge Patty beat Frank Sedgman, 6-1, 8-10, 6-2, 6-3.

And here's who squashed whom in Squash:

National Women's Champion

1940 Cecile Bowes, Philadelphia.

1941 Cecile Bowes, Philadelphia.

1942-46 No Tournament.

1947 Anne Page Homer, Philadelphia.

1948 Cecile Bowes, Philadelphia.

1949 Janet Morgan, England.

1950 Jane Austin, Philadelphia.

National Men's Champion

1940 A. Willing Patterson, Philadelphia.

1941 Charles M. P. Britton, Philadelphia.

1942 Charles M. P. Britton, Philadelphia.

1943-45 No Tournament.

1946 Charles M. P. Britton, Philadelphia.

1947 Charles M. P. Britton, Philadelphia.

1948 Stanley W. Pearson Jr.,Philadelphia.

1949 H. Hunter Lott Jr., Philadelphia.

1950 Edward J. Hahn, Detroit.

Rodeo Champs

Bareback Riding

1940	Carl Dossey
1941	George Mills
1942	Louis Brooks
1943	Bill Linderman
1944	Louis Brooks
1947	Larry Finley
1948	Sonny Tureman
1949	Jack Buschbom
1950	Jim Shoulders

All Around

1940	Fritz Truan
1941	Homer Pettigrew
1942	Gerald Roberts
1943	Louis Brooks
1944	Louis Brooks
1947	Todd Whatley
1948	Gerald Roberts
1949	Jim Shoulders
1950	Harry Tompkins

Bull Riding

1940	Dick Griffith
1941	Dick Griffith
1942	Dick Griffith
1943	Ken Roberts
1944	Ken Roberts
1947	Wag Blessing
1948	Harry Tompkins
1949	Harry Tompkins
1950	Harry Tompkins

Other Sports have changed a ton since the 40's. The only difference in rodeo is the prize money paid for roping, bulldogging and riding. The horses and bulls are pretty much the same. The cowboys get paid a little more, but not much. Rodeoing remains a very high risk, low pay sport. You can bet your boots that Jim Shoulders and Harry Tompkins didn't get rich at it, nor will their young-uns. Stick with baseball, kids.

"Hey! What about Polo?"

Okay. The United States Open Polo Champions were:

1940	Aknusti
1941	Gulf Stream
1942-45	Not Contested.
1946	Mexico
1947	Old Westbury
1948	Hurricanes
1949	Hurricanes
1950	Bostwick

And our bowling heroes were:

BWAA Bowler of the Year
Men:

1942	Johnny Crimmins
1943	Ned Day
1944	Ned Day
1945	Buddy Bomar
1946	Joe Wilman
1947	Buddy Bomar
1948	Andy Varipapa
1949	Connie Schwoegler
1950	Junie McMahon

Women:

1948	Val Mikiel
1949	Val Mikiel
1950	Marion Ladewig

Major Golf Champions

The Masters

1940	Jimmy Demaret
1941	Craig Wood
1942	Byron Nelson
1943-45	No Tournament
1946	Herman Keiser
1947	Jimmy Demaret
1948	Claude Harmon
1949	Sam Snead
1950	Jimmy Demaret

PGA

1940	Byron Nelson
1941	Vic Ghezzi
1942	Sam Snead
1943	No Tournament
1944	Bob Hamilton
1945	Byron Nelson
1946	Ben Hogan
1947	Jim Ferrier
1948	Ben Hogan
1949	Sam Snead
1950	Chandler Harper

U.S. Open

1940	Lawson Little
1941	Craig Wood
1942-45	No Tournament
1946	Lloyd Mangrum
1947	Lew Worsham
1948	Ben Hogan
1949	Cary Middlecoff
1950	Ben Hogan

NCAA

1940	Dixon Brooke, Virginia
1941	Earle Stewart, LSU
1942	Frank Tatum Jr.
1943	Wallace Ulrich, Carleton
1944	Louis Lick, Minnesota
1945	John Lorms, Ohio St.
1946	George Hamer, Georgia
1947	Dave Barclay, Michigan
1948	Bob Harris, San Jose St.
1949	E. Harvie Ward, North Carolina
1950	Fred Wampler, Purdue

British Open

1940-45	No Tournament
1946	Sam Snead
1947	Fred Daly
1948	Henry Cotton
1949	Bobby Locke
1950	Bobby Locke

Ben Hogan won the 1950 U.S. Open at Merion Golf Club in Ardmore, Pennsylvania — but not without accident. A year earlier, Bantam Ben suffered what was considered a career-ending injury when his car hit a bus. His was one of sport's most amazing recoveries.

And one of the decade's best
amateur golfers was busy elsewhere, too.

Feb. 9, 1940	Joe Louis beat Arturo Godoy in a split decision in 15 rounds.
Mar. 29, 1940	Joe Louis knocked out Johnny Paycheck in the 2nd round.
June 20, 1940	Joe Louis beat Arturol Godoy by a TKO in the 8th round.
Dec. 16, 1940	Joe Louis beat Al McCoy by a TKO in the 6th round.
Jan. 31, 1941	Joe Louis knocked out Red Burman in the 5th round.
Feb. 17, 1941	Joe Louis knocked out Gus Dorazio in the 2nd round.
Mar. 21, 1941	Joe Louis beat Abe Simon by a TKO in the 13th round.
Apr. 8, 1941	Joe Louis beat Tony Musto by a TKO in the 9th round.
May 23, 1941	Joe Louis beat Buddy Baer by DQ in the 7th round.
June 18, 1941	Joe Louis knocked out Billy Conn in the 13th round
Sep. 29, 1941	Joe Louis beat Lou Nova by TKO in the 6th round.
Jan. 9, 1942	Joe Louis knocked out Buddy Baer in the 1st round.
May 27, 1942	Joe Louis knocked out Abe Simon in the 6th round.
	And then, Joe Louis went overseas to fight a war.
June 9, 1946	Joe Louis knocked out Billy Conn in the 8th round.
Sep. 18, 1946	Joe Louis knocked out Tami Mauriello in the 1st round.
Dec. 5, 1947	Joe Louis beat Jersey Joe Walcott in a split decision in 15 rounds.
June 25, 1948	Joe Louis knocked out Jersey Joe Walcott in the 11th round.
June 22, 1949	Joe Louis beat Jersey Joe Walcott in a unanimous decision in 15 rounds.
Aug. 10, 1949	Joe Louis beat Ezzard Charles by a TKO in the 8th round.
Oct. 14, 1949	Joe Louis knocked out Pat Valentino in the 8th round.

The richest and busiest golfer of the decade was Joe Louis. Joe played a lot of golf in Chicago in the forties and was good enough to carry a two handicap. Today, there's a Chicago course named in his honor; the Joe Louis the Champ Golf Club at 131st and Halsted. In addition to golf, Joe also found time to box. He held the world heavyweight championship for 11 years and nine months, from June of 1937 until March of 1949. He found time to defend his title 25 times and piled up a career record of 63 wins (49 by knockout) and three losses. His boxing and golfing careers were interrupted in the prime of his life by a call to active duty. Joe had no fights for four years, from May of 1942 to June of 1946.

Big Race Winners

The Kentucky Derby

1940	Gallahadion
1941	Whirlaway
1942	Shut Out
1943	Count Fleet
1944	Pensive
1945	Hoop Jr.
1946	Assault
1947	Jet Pilot
1948	Citation
1949	Ponder
1950	Middleground

The Indy 500

1940	Wilbur Shaw
1941	Floyd Davis and Mauri Rose
1942-45	No Race
1946	George Robson
1947	Mauri Rose
1948	Mauri Rose
1949	Bill Holland
1950	Johnnie Parsons

Whirlaway won the Kentucky Derby in 1941, and also the Preakness and Belmont. There were three more Triple Crown winners in the forties: Count Fleet in 1943, Assault in 46 and Citation in 48.

WINNER
GEORGE ROBSON
INDIANAPOLIS MOTOR SPEEDWAY
1946

George Robson won the Indy in 1946 in this Thome Engineering Special. His average speed was 114.820 MPH, and the pole winner (Cliff Bergere) posted a speed of 126.472 MPH, over 100 MPH slower than the 1995 speed and only 28 MPH faster than 1915's.

The decade's best athletes

Men		Women	
1940	Tom Harmon, Football	**1940**	Alice Marble, Tennis
1941	Joe DiMaggio, Baseball	**1941**	Betty Hicks Newell, Golf
1942	Frank Sinkwich, Football	**1942**	Gloria Callen, Swimming
1943	Gunder Haegg, Track	**1943**	Patty Berg, Golf
1944	Byron Nelson, Golf	**1944**	Ann Curtis, Swimming
1945	Byron Nelson, Golf	**1945**	Babe Didrikson Zaharias, Golf
1946	Glenn Davis, Football	**1946**	Babe Didrikson Zaharias, Golf
1947	Johnny Lujack, Football	**1947**	Babe Didrikson Zaharias, Golf
1948	Lou Boudreau, Baseball	**1948**	Fanny Blankers-Koen, Track
1949	Leon Hart, Football	**1949**	Marlene Bauer, Golf
1950	Jom Konstanty, Baseball	**1950**	Babe Didrikson Zaharias, Golf

Army's Glenn Davis *won the Maxwell Award in 1944, the Heisman in 1946 and was also named Athlete of the Year by the Associated Press in '46. Backfield-mate Felix "Doc" Blanchard won the Heisman in 1945, along with the Maxwell Award and the James E. Sullivan Award.*

The world's fastest human in 1948 was Harrison Dillard of the United States. He was the 100-meter race Olympics champion, winning with a time of 10.3, equalling Jesse Owens' Olympic record.

The James E. Sullivan Award

1940	Greg Rice, Track
1941	Leslie MacMitchell, Track
1942	Cornelius Warmerdam, Track
1943	Gilbert Dodds, Track
1944	Ann Curtis, Swimming
1945	Doc Blanchard, Football
1946	Arnold Tucker, Football
1947	John B. Kelly Jr., Rowing
1948	Bob Mathias, Track
1949	Dick Button, Skating
1950	Fred Wilt, Track

These boys could play some basketball.

1. Michael Jordan
2. Bill Russell
3. Magic Johnson
4. Kareem Abdul-Jabbar
5. Bob Petitt
6. Oscar Robertson
7. Jerry West
8. Elgin Baylor
9. Wilt Chamberlain
10. Larry Bird
11. Charles Barkley
12. Bob Cousy
13. Julius Erving
14. Dolph Schayes
15. John Havlicek

The greatest ever? *The 15 listed, headed by the guy pictured above. You're quite right. Michael Jordan did not play in the forties, nor did any of basketball's all-time greats. The great athletes of the forties opted for football and baseball.*

In the forties, college football became the nation's main game. It was also the birth of more than a few legends.

It was almost as if the football world had been waiting for a great war to really get the game to explode.

Sure, there had been stars up to now and plenty of great games and teams. But until 1944, not that many people paid that much attention.

Maybe it was the violence of war, or maybe it was just plain luck that suddenly a whole bunch of superior players hit the fields, but 1944 was the year when college football finally went big time.

In 1944, football was played on three major fronts: pro, college and military bases. Because of the war, teams from military bases added a whole new category. Since these teams were made up mostly of recruits from colleges, the military bases played the colleges and were even ranked with them.

Of the top 20 college football teams in 1944, half of those were, in fact, military bases. And the teams that played for the national championship were none less than Army and Navy. Army won, in the final regular game of the season, 23 to 7.

1944
College Football Final Rankings

1.	Army	9-0-0
2.	Ohio State	9-0-0
3.	Randolph Field	10-0-0
4.	Navy	6-3-0
5.	Bainbridge Navy Training	10-0-0
6.	Iowa Pre Flight	10-1-0
7.	USC	7-0-2
8.	Michigan	8-2-0
9.	Notre Dame	8-2-0
10.	March Field	7-0-2
11.	Duke	5-4-0
12.	Tennessee	7-0-1
13.	Georgia Tech	8-2-0
14.	Norman Pre-Flight	6-0-0
15.	Illinois	5-4-1
16.	El Toro Marines	8-1-0
17.	Great Lakes Naval Station	9-2-1
18.	Fort Pierce	8-0-0
19.	St. Mary's Pre-Flight	4-4-0
20.	Second Air Force	10-2-1

Ohio State's Les Horvath won the 1944 Heisman after a brilliant season at tailback for the Buckeyes. He gained 924 yards on 163 rushes and scored 12 touchdowns.

Major Bowls, Jan. 4, 1945

Rose:	USC 25, Tennessee 0
Orange:	Tulsa 26, Georgia Tech 12
Cotton:	Oklahoma A&M 34, TCU 0
Sugar:	Duke 29, Alabama 26

Elroy "Crazylegs" Hirsch, probably more than anybody, can tell you how the war impacted a young man's athletic career. This scenario is, admittedly, a bit atypical, because Elroy developed an incredible athletic portfolio during World War II.

Elroy started out at the University of Wisconsin in 1943 and gained over 200 yards and threw a touchdown pass in a 17 to 7 upset win over Ohio State. Then he enlisted in the Marines and was sent to Michigan as a V-12 officer candidate. He played football at Michigan. He also played on the 1944 Michigan basketball team that won the Big Ten championship. As a baseball pitcher, he struck out 12 in the game that won Michigan the Big Ten title. He also broad-jumped for the Michigan track team and in one meet beat the great Buddy Young of Illinois.

After all this, the Marines sent Elroy to Camp LeJune in North Carolina for a year and then to El Toro in California, where he played more football. And when the war ended, he still had college eligibility remaining at Wisconsin. He elected to turn pro instead, with the Chicago Rockets. After a brilliant pro career with the Rockets and the Los Angeles Rams, Elroy returned to Wisconsin to be athletic director.

This is "Crazylegs" *during his days as a Wisconsin Badger.*

Army sophomore Glenn Davis, *shown here gaining yards against Columbia. Classmate and teammate Doc Blanchard and Notre Dame's Bob Kelly joined Horvath in the 1944 All American backfield.*

The 1940 Heisman winner was halfback Tom Harmon of Michigan. *Runner-up was John Kimbrough of Texas A&M. Harmon was the runner-up in 1939, to Nile Kinnick of Iowa. In the 1940 season, Harmon rushed 191 times for 852 yards and scored 16 touchdowns. Harmon also won the Maxwell award in 1940.*

187

Bruce Smith, University of Minnesota halfback, won the Heisman in 1941.
Runner-up was Angelo Bertelli of Notre Dame. Smith's team won the national championship that year, for the second year in a row. Minnesota's record was 8-0-0, the same that it was in 1940. Bernie Bierman was the Minnesota coach. For the 1941 season, Smith had 98 runs from scrimmage for 480 yards. He scored six touchdowns.

The 1942 Heisman winner was tailback Frank Sinkwich of Georgia. *Runner-up was quarterback Paul Governali of Columbia. Sinkwich was a great runner and passer. He completed 84 out of 166 passes for 1392 yards and 10 touchdowns. Governali won the Maxwell Trophy that year.*

Anybody know what's happened
to Vincent Banonis?

Steve was a center for the University of Detroit in 1941. He made All American. Then he joined the service and played for the Iowa Seahawks. After the war, he joined the Chicago Cardinals, where he starred at both center and linebacker. He finished his career with the Detroit Lions. He was last spotted at T.J. Moran's Ruth's Chris restaurant in Southfield, Mi. If anyone knows Steve's whereabouts, please get in touch with him and have him contact the publishers. We have a gift for him. Thank you.

Army's Mr. Inside and Mr. Outside:
The most devastating 1-2 backfield combination in college football history

If you're a football fan who grew up in the forties and if the sheer mention of those two legends of college football doesn't still send shivers up your spine, then you'd best book an appointment with your doctor. You've got Alzheimer's.

In 1944, 45 and 46, the Black Knights of the Hudson were a glorious back-home inspiration to the officers who were leading Americans to battle in World War II. Their games were broadcast to troops worldwide and they'd often find congratulatory telegrams after games from guys in the "Long Gray Line"... guys like General Dwight Eisenhower and General Douglas MacArthur. The young Cadets' turns would surely come in future battles of war, but until then they were destined to lead their country in the game of football. And the two future officers who answered that charge magnificently were Felix "Doc" Blanchard and Glenn Davis, also known to everybody with but a miniscule of gridiron memory as Mr. Inside and Mr. Outside.

Davis was called Mr. Outside because he could turn the corner and find daylight better than anyone who'd ever played before him, and maybe even since. That is arguable, for sure, but there are some college records Mr. Davis still owns today, some 50 years after he played, that are exceptional support for argument openers. Davis still has the NCAA highest career average gain per rush: 8.26 yards. He's tied with two others for most NCAA games with two or more touchdowns: 17. And he's tied with two others for the NCAA's most games scoring touchdowns: 31.

Davis was a great athlete. At 5-feet-9-inches, he weighed only 170 pounds. But he was bullet fast. Bill Yeoman, the former University of Houston coach who blocked for Davis and Blanchard their senior year, said this about them: "Everything they wrote about Blanchard was true. They never invented words to describe what Davis could do."

Blanchard was as devastating running through people as Davis was running by them. He played at 6-feet and 210 and just could not be stopped. He was also a great defensive player. He and Davis still hold the NCAA record for most career touchdowns by two players on the same team: 97. Blanchard accounted for 38 of those. They also hold the NCAA record for most points by two players from the same team: 585. Blanchard accounted for 231 of those.

Davis and Blanchard made Army one of college football's all-time great teams. In the three years they played, Army rolled to a 27-0-1 record. The tie was with the post-war all-stars of Notre Dame in 1946. So much for Army being a wartime fluke.

When Blanchard won the Heisman in 1945, Davis was second. Davis then won it in 1946. They're the only members of the same backfield to win the honor.

Both these college football heroes did fulfill their military obligations. Davis served in Korea while Blanchard joined the Air Force and won a Distinguished Flying Cross after flying 85 combat missions over North Viet Nam in 1967 and 68.

Glenn W. Davis and Felix A. "Doc" Blanchard, *1948 graduates of the United States Military Academy. Davis is on the left. Blanchard was inducted into the College Football Hall of Fame in 1959, Davis in 1961.*

Football under Frank Leahy:
Just how good was Notre Dame in the forties?

In the 1940s, the game of football found its Camelot in South Bend, Indiana. In that decade, Notre Dame was so good, a Notre Dame loss on Saturday was a major headline in every paper in America on Sunday.

Notre Dame finished in the top 10 an awesome total of nine times in that decade, with one third place finish, two seconds and four national championships–producing three of the 10 Heisman Trophy winners, two Outland Trophy winners, dozens of All Americans and 10 National Football Foundation Hall of Famers. And the coach, Frank Leahy, racked up a record unmatched by anybody in history–including that of his coach, the immortal Knute Rockne.

Coach Frank Leahy *with one of his 13 consensus All Americans, center and linebacker Jerry Groom, with team mascot Clashmore Mike III. Known as the "Iron Man," Groom regularly played 60 minutes a game for Leahy and helped Notre Dame compile an astounding 28-0-1 record his first three seasons. He was the Irish captain his senior year, in 1950.*

Leahy took over as head football coach and athletic director at Notre Dame in 1941. He was 33 years old but had already tasted the sweetness of success in South Bend. He was a starting tackle on Rockne's 1929 team that claimed the national title. His mission was simple: to repeat that accomplishment.

Leahy's 1941 Fighting Irish finished third in the country, with no losses and one tie–to Army, 0 to 0. They were sixth in 1942, with two losses and a tie. In 1943, they finished first. They lost once, on a 46-yard pass in the final 30 seconds of the season, to a Great Lakes Naval Station team made up of college All Americans. One of the Great Lakes stars of that game was a former Notre Damer called up for active duty– Hall of Fame running back Emil "Red" Sitko.

The war claimed Leahy and most of his players in 1944 and 1945, but the men he left behind were still good enough to finish ninth both years. Then, Leahy came back in 1946 to start a streak that's never been equalled. For over four years, Notre Dame never lost a game. The Irish won the national championship in 1946 and 1947, finished second to Michigan in 1948 and first again in 1949. Counting the last two games of the '45 season, they went 38 games without a defeat, with only one tie–another 0-0 game with Army in 1946.

No matter how you assess Notre Dame in the forties, the facts are astounding. Every year, except for the two war years, over 100 of the best football players in America tried out for the team. A Notre Dame letter (or monogram, if you will) was highly sought after–and even denied to many great footballers. In 1946, when dozens of war veterans came back to South Bend to join the returning lettermen and the incoming high school All Americans, competition was never as fierce anywhere. The returning starter at center, Bill

Walsh, suddenly found himself playing behind All American George Strohmeyer and Marty Wendell. Eleven of the 14 players out for starting guard positions had previously won Notre Dame letters. Six had earned two. Of the 14 tackle candidates, six had earned letters in previous years. And that list didn't include future Outland Trophy winner George Connor, who had already earned a distinction as the best lineman in the East when he played for Holy Cross. He'd also played two years of service football.

In those days, not even the pros could have handled Notre Dame. There were four Notre Damers on the 1946 All American team–John Mastrangelo at right guard, George Strohmeyer at center, George Connor at left tackle and John Lujack at quarterback. In 1947, 14 Notre Damers were picked for the College All Star game that was played the following summer. Five backs were chosen: John Lujack, Bob Livingstone, Bill Gompers, Pete Ashbaugh and Floyd Simmons. The nine linemen were: George Connor, Ziggie Czarobski, Joe Signaigo, Art Statuto, Zeke O'Connor, Gasper Urban, George Sullivan, George Strohmeyer and Bucky O'Connor. Frank Leahy was the coach. Every player but Bucky O'Connor went on to play pro ball, where they were joined by 1947 teammates Corwin Clatt and Frank Kosikowski.

There were some great players who couldn't even make the Notre Dame traveling squad in 1947. One of the players out for a guard position on the 1947 team was George "Cud" Tobin, who lettered in 1942 and starred on a great Iowa Pre-Flight team in 1943. He did not get his Notre Dame letter in 1946 and left to play for the New York Giants in 1947. There, he made the first team. Another returning player was center Art Statuto. He came back to Notre Dame in 1946 and was playing first string in spring practice. That autumn, when all the vets were back, Art found himself playing on fourth string, behind All American George Strohmeyer, All American Marty Wendell and Bill Walsh, the Notre Dame starter in 1945, 1947 and 1948. In 1946, Art did not win a letter at Notre Dame. But this Irish fourth-stringer did play in that 1947 College All Star game and was drafted by the Buffalo Bills, where he started for several years. He was later drafted by the Los Angeles Rams and made All Pro. Another outstanding pro who couldn't make the Notre Dame team in 1946 or 1947 was William "Zeke" O'Connor, who played on the 1948 College All-Star team and started at end for Buffalo and also played for the Cleveland Browns, New York Yankees and the Toronto Argonauts. At Notre Dame, he played behind All American Jim Martin, an All-Service player named Frank Kosikowski, All-American and Heisman winner Leon Hart– and several other seasoned players.

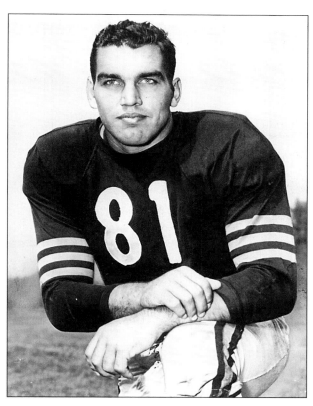

George Connor, *Notre Dame tackle, won the Outland Trophy in 1946.*

Competition was also brutal in the Notre Dame backfields of the forties, especially at quarterback. From 1941 through 1949, there were All Americans calling Notre Dame signals nearly every year. It started in 1941, when Coach Leahy needed a passer. He found him in the person of one Angelo Bertelli, who was then a seventh-string sophomore halfback. Leahy promoted Bertelli and the following year Angelo finished sixth in the voting for the Heisman. The next year, 1943, Angelo was able to play only six games for the Irish. He was called to active duty. But he still won the Heisman that year. His replacement that year was John Lujack. When Lujack was also called into the service, he was replaced by Frank Dancewicz. Frank was the 1945 All American quarterback. In 1946, Lujack was back and good enough to be a consensus All American and finish third in the Heisman. He won it in 1947. His backup in 1946 was George Ratterman, who was good enough to start for the College All Stars that following summer. Frank Tripucka was the Irish quarterback in 1948. He had an outstanding season, and Leahy loved to brag on him. He called Tripucka the best ball-handling, faking quarterback he ever had. Tripucka did not make All America, mainly because there just wasn't room for five Notre Damers on that year's dream team–Bill Fischer and Leon Hart were on it for the second straight year and were joined by Red Sitko and Marty Wendell. Fischer won the Outland Trophy that year. The 1949 Irish quarterback was Bob Williams. He made the All America team, along with teammates Red Sitko, Jim Martin and Leon Hart. Williams would become the sixth Notre Dame quarterback to be elected to the Hall of Fame. His favorite end, Leon Hart, won the Heisman.

Imagine, if you will, coming in from Iowa to join this star-studded group as a wide-eyed freshman just out of high school. That would be Jerry Groom, in 1947. His first drill: "They put me in a box for tackling practice and had the backs come at me one after another. First, Red Sitko. Then, John Panelli, then Billy Gompers, then Coy McGee, then Bob Livingston. Then, we scrimmaged, and I'm playing against guys like George Connor, George Strohmeyer, Marty Wendell, Joe Signaigo, George Sullivan and the rest of those guys." Young Mr. Groom did acquit himself well enough to make that team. And he went on to make All America and the Hall of Fame. Jerry began his fourth season at Notre Dame undefeated and was named captain of the 1950 team.

In the seven years that Leahy coached Notre Dame in the forties, his teams lost but three games. That was indeed the golden era of college football.

The Leahy Decade: Four national championships, two seconds and a third...three Heismans, two Outland Trophys, 10 Hall of Famers and dozens of All Americans

Leon Hart, *Notre Dame end, won the Heisman in 1949 and the AP male athlete of the year award.*

Angelo Bertelli, *Notre Dame quarterback, won the Heisman in 1943.*

Johnny Lujack, *Notre Dame quarterback, won the Heisman in 1947 and the AP male athlete of the year award.*

After four straight undefeated seasons, *a rare event occurred in South Bend, Indiana on October 7, 1950. Notre Dame lost, to cross-state rival Purdue. Helping to spoil the Irish record of no defeats since 1945 were quarterback Dale Samuels (10), and Mike Laccioli (21), (extreme right). This pass was good for 14 yards, and Purdue went on to win, 28 to 14.*

Up in Ann Arbor, mighty Michigan had a decade to remember, too.

The Wolverines started the 40s with the country's best player and went on to win four Big 10 titles and a national championship.

Michigan's record for the forties: 73-15-2.

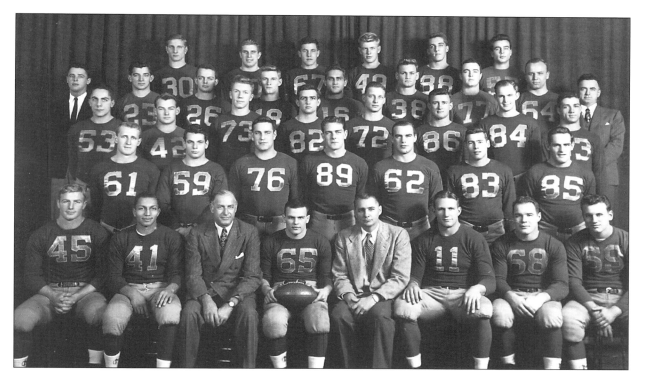

The 1948 Michigan team *owns the distinction of being the last Michigan team to finish unbeaten, untied and national champs. The other Michigan teams to achieve perfection were before them; the unbeaten national champs of 1901, 1902, 1932 and 1933. The 1947 Michigan team was 9-0-0, but finished second to Notre Dame for the national championship. Hail to Michigan!*

For two years, 'ol 98, *Tommy Harmon, electrified the nation with dazzling runs. As a junior in 1939, Harmon was runner-up for the Heisman. He won it in 1940, along with the prestigious Maxwell Award.*

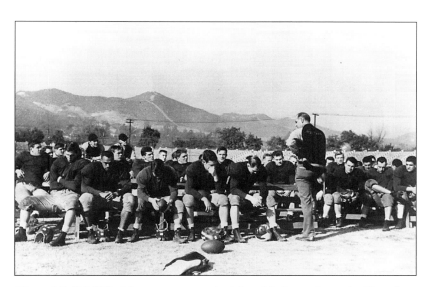

The 1947 Michigan team, *led by All American halfback and Heisman runner-up Bob Chappius, went undefeated and finished second to Notre Dame. Here they are getting ready for the 1948 Rose Bowl, at which they clobbered USC, 49 to 0.*

198

Doak Walker, Southern Methodist halfback, won the Heisman in 1948, beating out Charlie "Choo Choo" Justice of North Carolina. Walker had two great seasons at SMU. In 1947, he won the Maxwell Trophy. SMU went to the Cotton Bowl in Walker's junior and senior seasons, tieing Penn State, 13-13, and beating Oregon, 31-13. For the 1948 season, Walker gained 532 yards on 108 carries. He scored eight touchdowns.

199

North Carolina halfback Charlie "Choo Choo" Justice *was runner-up for the Heisman in 1948 and 49, even though he had much a much better record than the winners. He gained 5,000 rushing yards at North Carolina and punted for a 42.6-yard average in leading the Tarheels to ninth in the nation in 1947, third in 48 and 16th in 49. He then played in the 1949 East West Shrine Game and was runner-up for MVP. The following summer, he played in the College All Star Game and was again runner-up for MVP. Poor 'ol Charlie never got his just rewards prophesied in the song written about him: "All the Way, Choo Choo."*

Who else was No. 1 in
college football in the forties

National Champs

1940   Minnesota, 8 and 0 (Coach: Bernie Bierman)

1941   Minnesota, 8 and 0 (Coach: Bernie Bierman)

1942   Ohio State, 9 and 1 (Coach: Paul Brown)

1943   Notre Dame, 9 and 1 (Coach: Frank Leahy)

1944   Army, 9 and 0 (Coach: Red Blaik)

1945   Army, 9 and 0 (Coach: Red Blaik)

1946   Notre Dame, 8 and 0 and 1 (Coach: Frank Leahy)

1947   Notre Dame, 9 and 0 (Coach: Frank Leahy)

   Michigan, 10 and 0 (Coach: Fritz Crisler

1948   Michigan, 9 and 0 (Coach: Bennie Oosterbaan)

1949   Notre Dame, 10 and 0 (Coach: Frank Leahy)

Heisman Winners

1940   Tom Harmon, Michigan HB...John Kimbrough of Texas A&M was second.

1941   Bruce Smith, Minnesota HB...Angelo Bertelli of Notre Dame was second.

1942   Frank Sinkwich, Georgia HB...Paul Governali of Columbia was second.

1943   Angelo Bertelli, Notre Dame QB...Bob Odell of Pennsylvania was second.

1944   Les Horvath, Ohio State QB...Glenn Davis of Army was second.

1945   Doc Blanchard, Army FB...Glenn Davis of Army was second.

1946   Glenn Davis, Army HB...Charley Trippi of Georgia was second.

1947   John Lujack, Notre Dame QB...Bob Chappius of Michigan was second.

1948   Doak Walker, SMU HB...Charlie Justice of North Carolina was second.

1949   Leon Hart, Notre Dame End...Charlie Justice of North Carolina was second.

Not everyone who starred in the NFL in the 50s and 60s was a college hero in the 40s. Notable among that group was Hall of Famer Dick (Night Train) Lane, who played one year at Scottsbluff Junior College in Nebraska and then spent four years in the service playing service ball (at Fort Ord, California). Then, he worked as a laborer in an aircraft factory, stuffing slabs of oil-soaked metal into bins. Disgusted with that work, he walked into the offices of the L.A. Rams in 1952, got a tryout and then spent the next 14 years becoming one of the best defensive backs in NFL history. He finished as an All Pro with Detroit. His career total of 68 interceptions ranks third in all-time stats, behind Paul Krause and Emlen Tunnell.

Scottsbluff JC? You could win a couple beers with this info. Hey, you're welcome.

In 1929, Amos Alonzo Stagg had already earned himself the title Grand Old Man of Football. That year was his 38th season as head coach of the University of Chicago. He was 67 years old. He's the one without a necktie. The oldtimers sitting with him on the bench as guests at the 1929 Chicago-Wisconsin game–Dr. Ralph Hammill, Capt. W. S. Kennedy and Jonathan Webb–played for Stagg from 1896 to 99 and won the western championship in 1899. Little did these formers players know that Mr. Stagg was a long, long way from being through. Mr. Stagg went on to coach football for 31 more years.

In the Forties, the Grand Old Man of Football was still going strong.

At the ripe old age of 81, ordinary mortals are content to sit in the sun on front porches in rocking chairs and watch the world go by. But Amos Alonzo Stagg was far from ordinary, even at age 81. That was back in 1943 and this venerable coach was given a rare tribute by peers that included such coaching legends as Paul Brown, Lynn "Pappy" Waldorf, Bernie Bierman, Frank Leahy, Red Blaik, Fritz Crisler and Bennie Oosterbaan. For that year, they chose Mr. Stagg NCAA Coach of the Year.

The honor was not a gratuitous gift to a doddering old codger. Mr. Stagg's coaching performance in 1943 was the stuff legends are made of, and this sprightly old gent was already well familiar with the rarified air of that distinction.

Born when the American Civil War was going on, in 1862, Amos had to wait until he was in his late twenties to go off to college. It took him several years to earn enough money to pay for it. He elected to go to Yale, and when he got there he wanted to play football. There was a problem. Yale was short on coaches. So Amos pulled double duty. He became a player-coach. As a player, he did well enough to be named to the first All American football team. He was 27 years old and the year was 1889.

As a coach, Amos did well enough to get himself a full-time job on the Yale coaching staff. But first, he wanted to play some basketball. The problem there was the game hadn't been invented yet. So he went over the Springfield, Mass. and hooked up with a fellow named James Naismith. At a training center at the local YMCA, they put on a game. Naismith gets credit for inventing the game. Amos gets a slot in history for playing in the first basketball game. That was in 1891. Amos was 29.

Eddie LeBaron was 19 *in 1949. Amos Alonzo Stagg, the coach who recruited him, was 87.*

After that historic game, young James thanked young Amos for the help. Amos then headed back to New Haven. Basketball was going to be all right. But he was going to spend his life coaching football.

It did not take long for Amos to establish his credentials. Before the turn of the century, his University of Chicago squad won the western championship. That was his 1899 team. He won his first national football championship with the Maroons in 1905.

Mr. Stagg stayed at Chicago for over 40 years and became one of the most respected coaches in the country. He was very innovative and the modern game owes much to his inventions. He was also a master recruiter and motivator. He had high principles. He disdained smoking, drinking and cussing. "Double jackass" was as low as he sank when it came to cussing. When he was 73 years old, one of his halfbacks, Jay Berwanger, won the first Heisman Trophy.

Figuring that Mr. Stagg was now too old to coach, Chicago retired him. And when 1943 rolled around, Chicago was no longer playing football. But Mr. Stagg was still coaching it. He had taken the head coaching job at tiny College of Pacific, in Stockton, California. It took but a few seasons for Stagg to develop a winning program. In 1943, a year dominated by service teams, his Pacific team finished 19th in the nation.

Mr. Stagg still wasn't through. In 1946, when he was 84, he was one of the best recruiters in the country. He put together a squad good enough to set an NCAA season scoring record by the time they were seniors. That was the 1949 Pacific team that went undefeated. It was ranked tenth in the country and was led by future Washington Redskin quarterback Eddie LeBaron and San Francisco 49er tackle Don Campora, two of the players Stagg recruited. LeBaron finished sixth in Heisman voting that year.

After putting Pacific in the big time, Mr. Stagg finally retired from head coaching. But he signed on as an assistant at nearby Stockton Junior College and continued to coach until 1960. In his head coaching career, he won 314 games. Counting the 1949 Pacific team that he recruited, he had six undefeated seasons.

Mr. Stagg is the only person elected to both college football and basketball Halls of Fame. And he's the only one in football's Hall as both player and coach. He was unique. Grand is an apt description. In his book Touchdown, written in 1927, he wrote, "Winning isn't worthwhile unless one has something finer and nobler behind it.' As for innovations in the game, Knute Rockne claimed: "All football comes from Stagg."

Mr. Stagg did not retire to his rocking chair until he was 98. He died at 103.

In 1930, the Grand Old Man of Football *addressed a new squad of collegiate footballers for the 39th time in his career. It was a ritual Mr. Stagg would repeat 29 more times.*

All American Eddie LeBaron led Pacific to a 10-0-0 season in 1949.

Hall of Famer Gino Marchetti was a sophomore at USF in 1949.

Emlen Tunnell played for the Coast Guard and the University of Iowa before becoming the first black to play for the New York Giants, in 1948.

Total offense leaders in the forties

		Plays	Yards
1940	Johnny Knolla, Creighton	298	1420
1941	Bud Schwenk, Washington-MO	354	1928
1942	Frank Sinkwich, Georgia	341	2187
1943	Bob Hoernschemeyer, Indiana	355	1648
1944	Bob Fenimore, Oklahoma A&M	241	1758
1945	Bob Fenimore, Oklahoma A&M	203	1641
1946	Travis Bidwell, Auburn	339	1715
1947	Fred Enke, Arizona	329	1941
1948	Stan Heath, Nevada-Reno	233	1992
1949	Johnny Bright, Drake	275	1950

The Rose Bowl in the forties

1940	USC 14, Tennessee 0
1941	Stanford 21, Nebraska 13
1942	Oregon St. 20, Duke 16
1943	Georgia 9, UCLA 0
1944	USC 29, Washington 0
1945	USC 25, Tennessee 0
1946	Alabama 34, USC 0
1947	Illinois 45, UCLA 14
1948	Michigan 49, USC 0
1949	Northwestern 20, California 14
1950	Ohio State 17, California 14

1949 Associated Press College Football Rankings

1. **Notre Dame**   9-0-0
2. **Oklahoma**   10-0-0
3. **California**   10-0-0
4. **Army**   9-0-0
5. **Rice**   9-1-0
6. **Ohio State**   6-1-2
7. **Michigan**   6-2-1
8. **Minnesota**   7-2-0
9. **LSU**   8-2-0
10. **Pacific**   10-0-0
11. **Kentucky**   9-2-0
12. **Cornell**   8-1-0
13. **Villanova**   8-1-0
14. **Maryland**   7-1-0
15. **Santa Clara**   7-2-1
16. **North Carolina**   7-3-0
17. **Tennessee**   7-2-1
18. **Princeton**   6-3-0
19. **Michigan State**   6-3-0
20. **Missouri**   7-3-0
      Baylor   8-2-0

Army's Glenn Davis *won the Maxwell Award in 1944, the Heisman in 1946 and was also named Athlete of the Year by the Associated Press in '46. Backfield-mate Felix "Doc" Blanchard won the Heisman in 1945, along with the Maxwell Award and the James E. Sullivan Award.*

In 1949, the best in the west were the best there ever was.

Hurryin' Hugh McElhenny was up at the University of Washington, and they appreciated him so much that it was believed that when he turned pro, with the San Francisco 49ers, he took a cut in salary. And speaking of the 49ers, John Brodie and Joe Montana and Steve Young weren't the only great quarterbacks to lead that team. In 1949, it was Frankie Albert. And his fullback was one of the best ever, Joltin' Joe Perry. Joe's still ranked 12th on the all time NFL rushing list. With McElhenny, Albert and Perry, the 49ers had an All Pro backfield.

As great as the 49ers were, they had lots of competition. Across the bridge, in Berkeley, the University of California had an unbeaten team in 1949. Cal had hired Lynn "Pappy" Waldorf away from Northwestern, and Pappy quickly put together a powerhouse. The line was led by three All Americans. Guard Rod Franz made that distinguished team for a third straight year and was joined on it in 1949 by guard Forrest Klein and tackle Jim Turner. But it was the backfield that really spoiled Cal fans back then. All Americans Jackie Jensen (who became a great major league baseball star) and Jim Monachino were the halfbacks. Coming off the bench that year were backs Jackie Swaner, Pete Schabarum, Charley Sarver, Frank Brunk, Billy Main, Staten Webster and freshman Johnny Olszewski. Johnny O had to wait two years to win his All American honors. These backs kept kicker Jim "Truck" Cullom busy; he kicked 103 extra points between 1947 and 49, including 39 in 1949.

Hugh McElhenny, University of Washington fullback, being downed by Paul Baldwin, University of California halfback, after a two-yard gain in the second quarter of the game played at Berkeley, Calif., on Oct. 29, 1949. Cal won on its way to an unbeaten season.

The 1949 Cal quarterback, Bob Celeri, would have been an All American, if it weren't that many didn't think he was even the best quarterback in the state. Down at Loyola of Los Angeles there was a really good one named Don Klosterman. Over in Stockton was an even better one: College of Pacific's Eddie LeBaron. Eddie led Pacific to a 10-0 season, setting an NCAA team scoring record in the process. Eddie was recruited by the Grand Old Man of Football, Amos Alonzo Stagg. Eddie finished sixth in the Heisman and later replaced none less than Sammy Baugh in the pros and led the NFL in passing in 1958. And just across the state line was Stan Heath at the University of Nevada. Legend has it that he could throw the ball the length of the field.

There was another very good quarterback right in town: Ed Brown of the University of San Francisco. And by 1951, Brown's college team was even better than Cal's Golden Bears. Including Coach Joe Kuharich and Berl Tolar, who became the first black pro ref and publicist Pete Rozelle, 12 from that USF squad ended up in the NFL. Four, including NFL Commissioner Rozelle and players Ollie Matson, Gino Marchetti and Bob St. Clair, made the NFL Hall of Fame. Tackle Mike Mergen played for the Chicago Cardinals, end Ralph Thomas, guard Lou Stevens and halfback Joe Scudero played for the Washington Redskins and guard Dick Stanfel was All Pro five times with the Detroit Lions. And QB Brown played eight years with the Chicago Bears. Hey, we're talking football history here!

Jim "Truck" Cullum, *Cal tackle and placekicker.*

Bob Celeri, *Cal's almost All American quarterback.*

Jim Turner, *Cal tackle and 1949 All American.*

Jim Monachino, *Cal halfback and leading rusher.*

Lynn "Pappy" Waldorf, *Cal's head coach.*

Johnny Olszewski,
Cal's freshman fullback.

Forrest Klein,
*another of Cal's
All American
guards.*

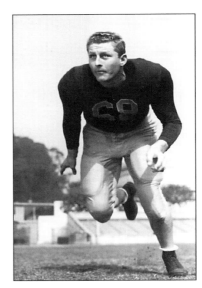

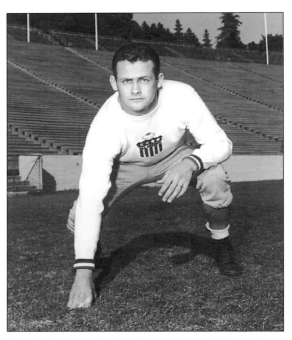

Rod Franz, *Cal's three-time All American guard.*

Jackie Jensen,
*Cal's All American
halfback.*

211

The pros also played some football in the forties.
A couple played it better than anybody before or since.

You talk to Sammy Baugh nowadays, down there at his cattle ranch outside Rotan, Texas, and ask him what it's like to be a football legend and he'll roll his eyes, spit a little tobacco juice into a plastic cup and drawl, "Hell, I was just one of the damned players." Well, according to the experts, he's a bit more than that. According to many, including contemporary quarterback Sid Luckman, the great Chicago Bear player, and sportswriter Mickey Herskowitz and author Beau Riffenburgh,who wrote *The Official NFL Encyclopedia*, Sammy Baugh is the greatest football player of all time, period.

In 1943, Sammy had the best season of any football player in history. Now that pro football is a game for specialists, his all-around records for that season will never be beaten. That year, Slingin' Sammy topped the NFL in passing with 1,754 yards and 23 touchdowns. He also led the league in interceptions. On offense, he threw 21. On defense, from his defensive halfback position, he led the league by intercepting 11, which he returned for 112 yards. He also led the league in punting, with a 45.9 average. Was that a misprint or a fluke? Nope. Sammy is the NFL's all-time career and season punting leader.

Baugh led the league in passing six times, more than anybody. And though he weighed only 180 pounds, Baugh played 16 seasons and was never seriously injured, though he usually played 60 minutes, no matter the game nor the score. In the off season, the bow-legged cowboy also played minor-league baseball for three years.

Sammy Baugh was indeed versatile. He was also superior at his different positions. In his NFL career, he played tailback as well as quarterback and made the All-NFL team three times as a halfback and only once as a quarterback. He was an exceptional tailback in the old single-wing offense. He was a great runner, blocker and passer. Yet, today, over 40 years after Sammy hung up his spikes,

At halfback or quarterback or defensive back or punter, *Sammy Baugh was the best ever.*

he's considered one of the greatest T-formation quarterbacks to ever play the game. And Washington didn't switch to the T until 1944, Sammy's eighth year in the league. He led the NFL in passing six times, in his rookie season in 1937 and five more times in the forties.

As a quarterback, Slingin' Sammy was at least the equal of Johnny Unitas, Otto

Graham and Joe Montana, the other quarterbacks selected by the NFL for the 75th anniversary all-time team. But those three were nowhere near Sammy's equal as a runner or blocker or defensive halfback. And as a punter, nobody's ever come close to him.

Baugh's Redskins won the NFL title in his rookie year of 1937. He was again set to throw in the 1940 championship game, but rarely had the ball as 10 Bears scored in the 73 to 0 Bear win. When asked what could have happened if one of his receivers hadn't dropped an early sure touchdown pass, Sammy replied in typical Baugh candor, "It would have been 73 to 7." His team got revenge by beating the Bears for the 1942 championship, 14 to 6. The Redskins then lost to the Bears in the 1943 title game when Sammy got kicked in the head making a tackle in the first half and sat out the second.

After his retirement, Baugh coached at Hardin Simmons and calf-roped on the rodeo circuit until 1975. He still plays a mean game of golf and has four holes-in-one.

The greatest receiver who ever played wore a leather helmet and high-top shoes.

In the 75-year history of the NFL, there have been hundreds of great wide receivers, many who have gained thousands of yards. Names like Art Monk, Steve Largent, Charlie Joiner, James Lofton and Jerry Rice come quickly to mind. But the man who invented the position is still universally considered the best of them all.

Don Hutson wasn't just a great end; he dominated his era like no other football player in history. The editors of *Sports Illustrated* named him their greatest player of all time, directly in front of Jim Brown, Otto Graham, Dick Butkus and Walter Payton.

Hutson played in the NFL from 1935 to '45, and no player ever had it more his way. In the 10 years that he played, he caught three times more touchdown passes (a total of 99) than No. two and nine times more than No. three.

Some have passed Hutson off as a war-time fluke. But he ruled the league for seven full seasons before any of his opponents went off to war.

As you should expect, Hutson had an auspicious beginning in the NFL. In his first play from scrimmage in the opening game in 1935, against the mighty Chicago Bears, he lined up split to the left. Johnny Blood was way out to the right. The Bears covered Blood as Hutson went downfield, faked the halfback out, cut back to the middle, ran past the safety, caught the ball on the Packer 43-yard line and ran it in. Until that moment, defenses didn't expect to see long passes attempted on the first play. From then on, they started looking for it, especially in the direction of Don Hutson.

In 11 seasons, *Don Hutson caught a lot of footballs*

Hutson had great speed. In college, at Alabama, he once left a baseball game to run the 100 in 9.8 seconds in a track meet, then returned to finish the baseball game. He also invented maneuvers that befuddled defenders. His repertoire of moves became so sophisticated, defenses never caught up to him.

Hutson also played defense in his early years in the pros, at right halfback. He was also a great blocker. But receiving was his forte, and during his career he led the NFL in receptions eight times. He also set a league record by catching at least one pass in 95 consecutive games (from 1937 to 45). That was a record that lasted 24 years. He was also the first receiver to top 1,000 yards in a season. He did that in 1942.

But the most amazing thing about Hutson was how much better he was than his competition. He led the league in receptions every year from 1941 to 45, averaging 57 catches per game when it was rare for anybody else to get half that many. In 1942, he obliterated NFL records by piling up 1,211 yards and 17 touchdowns on 74 catches. Runner-up Pop Ivy had but 27 receptions.

In 1944, Hutson almost singlehandedly broke the Chicago-Washington-New York NFL championship string, leading the Packers to their first title since 1939. With nothing left to prove and his place in football immortality secured, Hutson retired after the 1945 season.

In the fall of 1995, we roasted Elmer Angsman on his 70th birthday. And we presented him with a gift: a blow-up dinosaur.

Here's the roast:

Once upon a time, giant dinosaurs roamed the earth. And they vanished and after a while Elmer Angsman was born. That was a long time ago, too. It was well before the greatest depression in American history, four years before the Big Crash, long before saran wrap, in-line skates, hoola hoops, microwave ovens, gasoline lawn mowers, cellular telephones, electric garage door openers, the Kennedy Expressway, Schaumburg, motor scooter, airlines, and pay-per-view television...or for that matter, television of any sort.

Franklin Roosevelt was a junior congressman. Alf Landon was working on his master's and Adolph Hilter was a corporal in the German army. Hiro Hito was taking a beginner's karate class. Omar Bradley was teaching maneuvers at West Point. And it would be 19 years before the Dow Jones broke 150.

The year Elmer was born, Notre Dame took an unbeaten team to the Rose Bowl and beat Stanford, 27 to 10. The coach was Knute Rockne and the Irish backfield consisted of four guys named Stuhldreher, Crowly, Miller and Layden. Nobody would win the Heisman for 10 years, because it didn't exist back then. Felix "Doc" Blanchard wasn't born yet. Neither were Johnny Lattner, Paul Hornung, Billy Cannon and John Huarte. And Amos Alonzo Stagg was the grand *young* man of football.

Today, all of the running backs in the national Football League, there are very few who are white. Can you name *two?* Probably not. When Elmer played, you couldn't name a black running back. There were none.

When Elmer was a boy, he worked at Chicago's Union Stockyards. That's long since *vanished.*

Elmer played college ball for Notre Dame, back when they won all their games. And he played for a good coach. And his name wasn't Lou.

Elmer played pro ball for a team most NFL fans today have never heard of. A *Chicago* team that not only won, but won a world championship. And he practically played for free. Today, a place kicker makes 10 times more in one season than Elmer did in his entire career.

And Elmer *stayed* with the Chicago Cardinals. *For his entire career!*

Elmer...you've been around a while. You're a throwback, a bona fide living legend. A rompin' stompin Brontosaurus. We love you. Happy Birthday, pal.

The all-white 1947 NFL World Champion Chicago Cardinals. *Blacks wouldn't join the team until it became the St. Louis Cardinals. And a black pro footballer wouldn't come to Chicago until COP's Eddie Macon joined the Chicago Bears in 1951.*

The Dream Backfield of the 1947 NFL World Champion Chicago Cardinals consisted of Elmer Angsman, Paul Christman, Pat Harder and Charley Trippi. Many call it the greatest all-white backfield ever assembled.

A tale of two NFL cities: Chicago and Pittsburgh

Chicago

George Halas drove over to Canton, Ohio, in 1920 for a meeting with 11 other football fanatics in a motor car showroom. Little did he dream of how successful the new pro football league mapped out on the hood of a new Hupmobile would become. Nor did young George reckon on how much his $100 membership fee would eventually be worth.

In the beginning, these men did not set out to amaze the world. The biggest city asked to support their aspirations was Akron, Ohio. The rest of the league included such rural bastions as Canton, Hammond (Indiana), Rock Island (Ilinois) and Decatur (Illinois), which was George Halas's entry in the new league. Chicago, New York, Philadelphia and Washington were far beyond the ambitions of their infant organization.

It took a full season for the new league to gain enough of a foothold to move into the big time and the big cities. Halas moved his team to Chicago and in 1922 changed the name from the Chicago Staleys to the Chicago Bears. However, were it not for a few superior athletes who had caught the nation's fancy as college stars, the NFL may have indeed disappeared as quietly as it began. Jim Thorpe and Ernie Nevers were two of those. Harold (Red) Grange was another. Damon Runyan had knighted Grange by decreeing that "On the field, he is the equal of three men and a horse."

On November 21, 1925, the day after Grange's final collegiate game at the University of Illinois, he signed a pro contract with Halas. With Grange as his drawing card, Halas was now ready to take on Chicago and the world. A week later, big-time pro football officially began when the Chicago Bears went on the road to showcase their newest acquisition. The barnstorming tour began in St. Louis and Grange delighted some 8,000 nearly frozen fans by scoring four touchdowns. Three days later, Grange played before 35,000 in a Philadelphia rainstorm and scored both touchdowns in a 14 to 7 Bears win. By the time the Bears hit New York, the very next day, the American public was hooked. New York's 1925 debut in the fledgling NFL had been a dismal flop. When the Bears came to New York earlier, in the regular season, hardly anybody paid them much attention. But this time, the biggest crowd in pro football's young history came out to the Polo Grounds to watch the wet, tired Bears. Grange did not disappoint the 73,000 fans who paid good money to see him. He scored a touchdown to lead the Bears to a 19 to 7 win. That one game kept Giant owner Tim Mara from cashing in his franchise. Pro football was launched in New York and would soon captivate the rest of the country. In 12 days, Grange and the Bears played in eight cities. The tour was so successful, it was extended until late January throughout the south and then the west. Grange earned $100,000 for his efforts but Halas was an even bigger winner. He founded a sport for the ages.

By the time the forties rolled around, pro football was well on its way to being huge.

Maybe George Halas wasn't yet aware of the monster he'd created, but the rest of the world was. In the first 10 NFL championship games, from 1933 to 1944, the Bears were involved in seven. That included the historic 73 to 0 trouncing of Washington in 1940. After that, the Chicago Bears were known as The Monsters of the Midway.

Today, each of the 30 teams in the NFL is worth around $200 million. One team that is not for sale is the Chicago Bears, which is owned and operated by the children and grandchildren of George Halas. The Bears are still his baby. So is the NFL.

Pittsburgh

It has often been reported that one of fellows at that infamous meeting over the hoods and fenders of the Hupmobiles in Canton back there in 1920 was one Art Rooney. The rumor's false, folks. Rooney did not come into the league until 1932, when he had a big day at the track and used his winnings to buy a franchise for Pittsburgh. Incidentally, that was also the year that Halas became sole owner of the Bears.

Not only did Art not measure up to George Halas in NFL authorship and longevity, he also felt quite short in grit, loyalty and football smarts.

For a long, long time, George Halas was a winner. For a long, long time, Art Rooney was not. When the 1940 NFL Championship Game was played, Art was a spectator and watched in envy as Halas coached his Bears to the 73 to 0 rout of the Redskins.

Rooney did not picture the future of pro football nearly as clearly as did Halas. Papa George was forever strengthening the team and league image. He helped wrangle the first network deal for the league. That 1940 championship game was the first football game ever carried on network radio. The Mutual Broadcasting System paid $2,500 for the rights to air the game on 120 stations. Though this is peanuts compared to the million bucks per commercial charged for today's Super Bowl telecasts, it was a start.

Art Rooney, meanwhile, reacted to the Bears win in a bizarre fashion. Frustrated by years of losing, Art sold his Pittsburgh team to a fellow named Alexis Thompson for $180,000. Mind you, the worth of an NFL franchise has since escalated by at least three more zeroes on that figure.

Rooney did recover from that period of temporary stupidity. He bought a half interest in the Philadelphia Eagles. Then, homesick for Pittsburgh, he made a franchise switch with Thompson and moved himself and his team back to Pittsburgh.

It gets more bizarre. While Rooney's new Pittsburgh Steeler team wallowed in the NFL basement for decades, playboy Thompson (that's what the press wags tagged him) got his football act together. Thompson hired Earle (Greasy) Neale to coach his team and Neale found a quarterback named Thompson (Tommy: no relation) to run his T formation. Within three years, the Eagles were winning more than they were losing.

Then the war broke out. George Halas and some 600 other NFL players, coaches and officials were called to duty. Twenty one of those men never came home, including 12 active players.

When Halas returned, so did the Bears. With Halas at the helm again, the Bears whipped the Giants 24 to 14 in 1946 before a record NFL title game of 58,346 in the Polo Grounds. The Bears had also beaten the Giants, 37 to 9, to win the 1941 title. They lost to Washington in the 1942 finals and then beat Washington 41 to 21 to win the 1943 title. Green Bay won it in 1944 and Cleveland in 1945, as Rooney continued to watch.

Rubbing salt into Rooney wounds, the Thompson-Thompson Philadelphia team made it to the finals in 1947, losing to the Chicago Cardinals. Then the Eagles won it all in 1948 and 49. It would take 26 more years before Art Rooney's beloved Steelers would win a championship. That was finally accomplished in 1975, the 55th anniversary of the NFL, when his AFC Steelers beat the NFC Minnesota Vikings in Super Bowl IX, 16 to 6. His Steelers then won it three more times, in 1976 and in 1979 and 80. Way to hang in there, Art!

One of 23 Bears in the NFL Hall of Fame *is ol' No. 42, Sid Luckman, the man who first made the T formation work in the NFL. The brainchild of Ralph Jones, Clark Shaughnessy and George Halas, the Bears' T in 1940 featured many of the moves of today's modern pro set, and young QB Luckman was the perfect man to run it. Backs were going in motion and an end was split the other way. From this setup, Luckman could hand off on quick traps or counters or throw short passes to the flat, look-ins, deep, or the occasional seam pass off a quick drop to keep the defense honest. He did have it all perfected for the NFL Championship Game that year, when he directed the Bears to the famous 73 to 0 rout of the Redskins.*

Luckman played 12 seasons for the Bears, from 1939 to 50. He is the all-time Bear leader in attempts (1,774), completions (904), yards (14,686) and TDs (137). In a 1943 game against the New York Giants, he set an NFL record by throwing seven touchdown passes in a 56 to 7 Bear win. The Columbia University graduate led the Bears to four NFL titles and made All NFL five times. In 1943, he was league MVP. He was inducted into the NFL Hall of Fame in 1965 and the Bears have retired his number.

In 1940, rookie Chicago Bear halfback George McAfee *played in his first NFL Championship Game, against the Washington Redskins. In the play shown above, he gained seven yards. It was one of the shortest runs the Bears made all day. For the game, Bear backs rambled for 381 rushing yards and 10 different players scored touchdowns. The Monsters of the Midway were also monstrous on defense that day, intercepting eight passes, returning three for touchdowns, and holding the Redskins to only five yards by rushing. The final score was 73 to 0, still the largest margin in the history of the game.*

Ironically, had the game been close, McAfee probably would not have played. The Bears were so loaded with talent in 1940 and 41, he saw little playing time. Then he was in the Navy in World War II the next three seasons. But he came back and played superbly for six seasons, at halfback, punt returner and defensive back. He had 21 career interceptions and his career average of 12.78 yards on 112 punt returns is still the NFL record.

He was inducted into the NFL Hall of Fame in 1966 and ol' Number Five will never be worn by another Bear. George's number is one of 13 retired Bear numbers.

George Halas, *the man who helped create both the monster (the NFL) and the monsters (the Bears) led both the league and the team for more than half a century. He was one of the most enduring personalities in sports history.*

At the University of Illinois, he lettered in football, basketball and baseball. After graduation in 1918, he joined the Navy for the first of two tours of duty. He was named Player of the Game in the 1919 Rose Bowl, playing end on the Great Lakes team that beat the Marines 17 to 0. A commander when he left active duty in 1946, he retired as a captain in the Naval Reserve. He was awarded the Distinguished Citizen Award, the highest honor the Navy can bestow on a civilian.

After leaving the Navy the first time, Halas played right field for the New York Yankees, a position later taken by George Herman "Babe" Ruth. A hip injury ended his baseball career, but didn't stop him from playing football. After helping to organize the Bears and the NFL, he both coached and played for the Bears. He played end from 1920-29 and was named to the NFL All Pro squad of the 1920s. He coached the Bears to eight championships and retired in 1968 with a career record of 324 wins. He is a charter member of the NFL Hall of Fame.

By the 4th quarter of the 1940 NFL Championship Game, the Washington Redskins
starters watched in disbelief. The somber man with his chin on his hands is Sammy Baugh.

The one with the fist is George Connor. *After making All American and winning the Outland Trophy at Notre Dame, George Halas (who else?) drafted Connor to play for the Bears in 1948. Halas was not disappointed. Connor became one of the NFL's most feared defenders. In his eight seasons with the Bears, he put lots of hurt on lots of people. He was the first of the big, mobile and mean outside linebackers. He made All NFL five times, including both offense and defense in 1951 and 52. He was a tackle on offense, one of the best in his or any other era in pro football.*

George played in the first four Pro Bowls. In the 1952 game he made believers out of everybody. It was late in the game and the opposition was deep in his territory. He made a tackle for a loss on first down. He made a solo tackle on second down. He sacked the quarterback on third down. On fourth down he batted down a pass in the end zone. George is one of the 23 Chicago Bears in the NFL Hall of Fame

They called this man Bulldog. *Pit Bull would have been more descriptive. Clyde Turner got the nickname for work he did as a teenage cowboy in Sweetwater, Texas. After trading cattle and bulldogging steers for a year, he earned enough money to enter Hardin-Simmons College in Abilene, Texas. He tried out for center on the football team and was good enough to be drafted in the first round in 1940 by George Halas. This infuriated Detroit Lions owner George Richards, who thought he had a lock on Turner. He tried to get Turner to quit football for a year until Halas forgot about him, and then sign with the Lions. The league found out about the scheme and fined Richards $5,000 for tampering.*

Clyde "Bulldog" Turner played for Halas for 13 seasons. He was a flawless snapper and excellent blocker who was All NFL six times. He also played guard and tackle for the Bears. On defense, he played linebacker and led the league in 1942 with eight interceptions. He also played running back in emergency situations and scored on a 48-yard run in 1944. He also had a 96-yard return for a TD in 1947. He was inducted into the NFL Hall of Fame in 1966 and his number, 66, has been retired by the Bears.

In 1943, the Chicago Bears won the world championship *without their owner and coach, George Halas. He left for the Navy in 1942. Hunk Anderson and Luke Johnson co-coached the wartime Bears and made the missing-from-football-action Papa Bear very happy in 1943 with an 8-1-1 season, including a 41-21 get-even blasting of the Redskins for the title (the Redskins won it in 1942, 14 to 6). In the 1943 season Sid Luckman became the first pro to pass for over 400 yards in a game. He hit the Giants with 433 yards and seven TDs. In the championship game, he threw for five TDs. And Bronko Nagurski scored his last Bear TD on a three-yard run.*

Who led the NFL in the forties

Rushing

1940	Byron White	Det	146 Attempts	514 Yards	3.5 Average	5 TDs
1941	Clarence Manders	Bklyn	111 Attempts	486 Yards	4.4 Average	5 TDs
1942	Bill Dudley	Pitt	162 Attempts	696 Yards	4.3 Average	5 TDs
1943	Bill Paschal	NY	147 Attempts	572 Yards	3.9 Average	10 TDs
1944	Bill Paschal	NY	196 Attempts	737 Yards	3.8 Average	9 TDs
1945	Steve Van Buren	Phil	143 Attempts	832 Yards	5.8 Average	15 TDs
1946	Bill Dudley	Pitt	146 Attempts	604 Yards	4.1 Average	3 TDs
1947	Steve Van Buren	Phil	217 Attempts	1008 Yards	4.6 Average	13 TDs
1948	Steve Van Buren	Phil	201 Attempts	945 Yards	4.7 Average	10 TDs
1949	Steve Van Buren	Phil	263 Attempts	1146 Yards	4.4 Average	11 TDs

Passing

1940	Sammy Baugh	Wash	111 out of 177 for 1367 Yards	12 TDs	10 INTs
1941	Cecil Isbell	G. Bay	117 out of 206 for 1479 Yards	15 TDs	11 INTs
1942	Cecil Isbell	G.Bay	146 out of 268 for 2021 Yards	24 TDs	14 INTs
1943	Sammy Baugh	Wash	133 out of 239 for 1754 Yards	23 TDs	19 INTs
1944	Frank Filchock	Wash	84 out of 147 for 1139 Yards	13 TDs	9 INTs
1945	Sammy Baugh	Wash	128 out of 182 for 1669 Yards	11 TDs	4 INTs
	Sid Luckman	Chi	117 out of 217 for 1725 Yards	14 TDs	10 INTs
1946	Bob Waterfield	LA	127 out of 251 for 1747 Yards	18 TDs	17 INTs
1947	Sammy Baugh	Wash	210 out of 354 for 2938 Yards	25 TDs	15 INTs
1948	Tommy Thompson	Phil	141 out of 246 for 1965 Yards	25 TDs	11 INTs
1949	Sammy Baugh	Wash	145 out of 255 for 1903 Yards	18 TDs	14 INTs

Receiving

1940	Don Looney	Phil	58 Receptions for 707 Yards	12.2 Average	4 TDs
1941	Don Hutson	GB	58 Receptions for 738 Yards	12.7 Average	10 TDs
1942	Don Hutson	GB	74 Receptions for 1211 Yards	16.4 Average	17 TDs
1943	Don Hutson	GB	47 Receptions for 776 Yards	16.5 Average	11 TDs
1944	Don Hutson	GB	58 Receptions for 866 Yards	14.9 Average	9 TDs
1945	Don Hutson	GB	47 Receptions for 834 Yards	17.7 Average	9 TDs
1946	Jim Benton	LA	63 Receptions for 981 Yards	15.6 Average	6 TDs
1947	Jim Keane	Chi	64 Receptions for 910 Yards	14.2 Average	10 TDs
1948	Tom Fears	LA	51 Receptions for 698 Yards	13.7 Average	7 TDs
1949	Tom Fears	LA	77 Receptions for 1013 Yards	13.2 Average	9 TDs

Philadelphia's Steve Van Buren *led the NFL in rushing four times in the forties.*

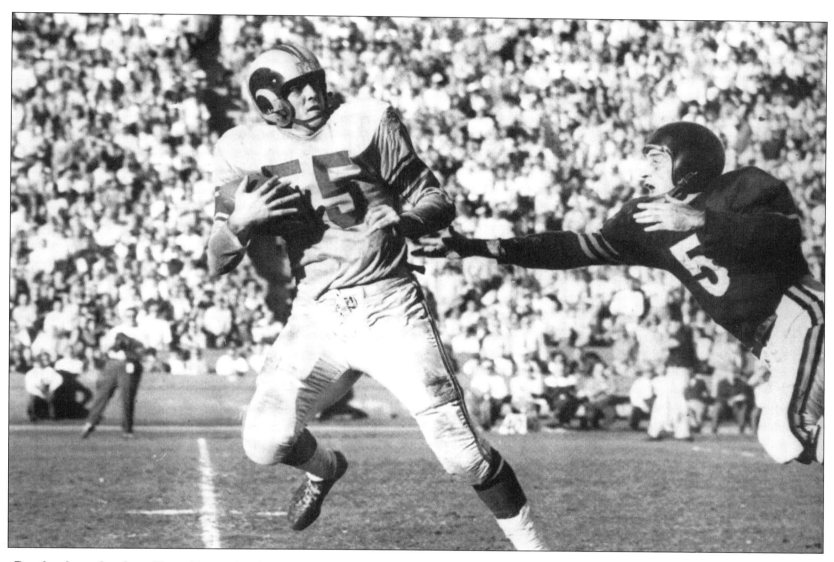

By the late forties, Tom Fears had replaced Don Hutson as the NFL's most feared receiver. He led the league in receptions in 1948 and 49 and in 1950 he set a record that stood for 10 years. In one game that season, against Green Bay, he caught 18 passes. Ram quarterbacks never had it so good. They also had "Crazylegs" Hirsch to catch their passes.

When these guys all get to heaven, they could beat anybody on earth.

Defense:

Safety
Emlen Tunnell

Defensive Backs
Night Trane Lane, Johnny Lujack, Sammy Baugh

Linebackers
Bulldog Turner, Chuck Bednarik, George Connor

Nose Guard
Bill Willis

Defensive Tackles
Leo Nomellini, Ernie Stautner, Arnie Weinmeister, Artie Donovan, Bucko Kilroy

Defensive Ends
Len Ford, Doug Atkins, Gino Marchetti

Punters
Sammy Baugh, Horace Gillom

Punt Returners
George McAfee, Emlen Tunnell, Bill Dudley, Charlie Trippi

Kickoff Returners
Lynn Chandnois, Buddy Young

Mel Hein *started for the Giants for 15 years and made All Pro eight consecutive years.*

Offense:

Quarterbacks

Sammy Baugh, Otto Graham, Frankie Albert, Sid Luckman, Bob Waterfield, Bobby Layne, Paul Christman, Cecil Isbell, Charlie Conerly

Running Backs

Steve Van Buren, Joe Perry, Bill Dudley, Bill Paschal, Marion Motley, Bronko Nagurski, Hugh McElhenny, Doak Walker, Charlie Trippi, Choo Choo Justice, Glenn Davis, Elmer Angsman, Pat Harder, Marshall Goldberg, Cliff Battles, Glenn Davis, George McAfee

Ends

Don Hutson, Dante Lavelli, Elroy Hirsch, Tom Fears, Leon Hart, Pistol Pete Pihos, Mac Speedie

Tackles

George Connor, Al Wistert, Joe Stydahar

Guards

Bruno Banducci, Danny Fortmann, George Musso, Bill Fischer

Centers

Clyde (Bulldog) Turner, Chuck Bednarik, Mel Hein, Frank Gatski, Jerry Groom

Placekickers

Lou Groza, George Blanda, Ben Agajanian

Coaches

George Halas, Paul Brown, Curly Lambeau

Chicago's Bronko Nagurski *played his last game for the Chicago Bears in 1943.*

Paul Brown *coached the Cleveland Browns for 17 years. He had but one losing season.*

In the early forties, this was the color of the athletes in the big leagues.

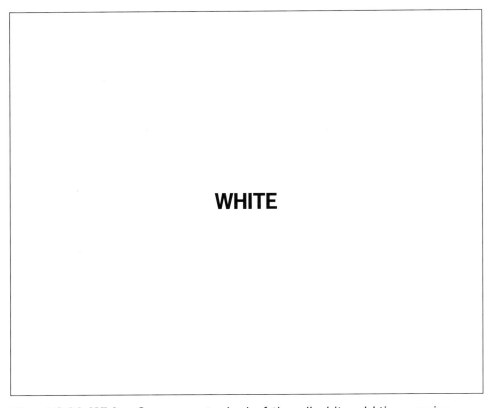

WHITE

The 1941 White Sox *were typical of the all-white old-time major league baseball players who performed out on the green grass under blue skies in the early forties. In 1944, the all-white St. Louis Cardinals beat the all-white St. Louis Browns to win the 1944 World Series. But, in three years, pro baseball's ban on blacks was history and a few years after that, so were the all-white Browns. In 1947, all-black Jackie Robinson joined the previously all-white Dodgers and the Browns became the Redbirds. And three blacks were soon playing for the Indians (the baseball team in Cleveland, not a red-skinned tribe on a western reservation).*

By the late forties, the players in the pros were white *and* black.

In 1946, Jackie Robinson *made baseball history. Jackie, pictured here with manager Leo Durocher, was the first black player in modern major league baseball. He was also one of the strongest competitors the game has ever known.*

Fullback Marion Motley *and guard Bill Willis made football history in 1946 by joining the Cleveland Browns of the All America Football Conference. Five years later, when the Browns were in the NFL, Motley was the unanimous choice as the NFL's all-star fullback.*

"Don't look back. Something may be gaining on you."– Satchel Paige, arguably the greatest pitcher baseball's ever known. Paige played in the Negro Leagues for 22 years with such black stars as Cyclone Bill Williams, Cool Papa Bell and Martin Dihigo. Of this group, only Paige ever made it to the majors. He got there in 1948, at age 42. Paige won 2,000 games and threw 45 no-hitters. He last pitched for Kansas City in 1965, at age 59.

A pro football dynasty started when 238-pound Marion Motley joined Edgar Jones, Lou Saban and Otto Graham of the Cleveland Browns. Here they are after routing Buffalo 49 to 7 to win the 1946 All American Football Conference Championship. The Browns went on to win five consecutive championships, including a 30 to 28 win over NFL rival Los Angeles Rams in 1950.

By the end of the forties, *many of the players crossing home plate in the big games in the majors were black players. Not only Jackie Robinson but also Roy Campanella, Luke Easter, Larry Doby and Satchel Paige had become familiar names in all American households.*

A few more things to tell the grandkids about the forties.

The forties version of the portable phone weighed 44 pounds. Postage stamps cost $.03 apiece. Bread was $.09 a loaf. Gas was $.21 a gallon. The average house cost $8,649. And the minimum wage was $.30 an hour. It would be 10 years before a cure for polio would be found.

Except for a few big band leaders, Joe Louis was the only black star on any stage in America for more than half the decade.

Major league baseball wasn't played any farther south (or west) than St. Louis.

There were no pro football teams down south, and only two out west (the Rams and 49ers).

Hockey was only played up north. Hardly anybody played soccer.

There was no TV.

And nobody wore a face mask.

"Hey! You forgot to mention:

Shaky Legs Corey,

VERNON Valdez,

Ish Castellano,

Vernon Ratkovich,

Kenny Uselton,

Kenny Cook,

Kenny Castle,

Davey One Eye Cox,

Stan Heath,

Ed Bagdon,

Paul Gerlach,

Clint Castleberry,

Bob Fenimore,

Joe Steffy,

the Human Stork,

Kevin Wade,

Billy O'Rourke

Ron Galiene,

Suitcase Simpson

and his little bro Briefcase,

Tiny and Steve Campora,

Joe DiTomaso,

Doug The Body Purl,

Artie Mesistrano,

Big Mike Dorroh and

Squermin' Herman Wedemeyer!"

Okay, guys. You got mentioned. Happy now?

Oldtimers Chapter

**"A little learning is a dangerous thing;
Drink deep or taste not the Pierian spring.
There shallow thoughts intoxicate the brain,
and drinking largely sobers us again."**

Alexander Pope, *An Essay on Criticism*

The point is, time's running out on all of us. So hurry up and learn everything you can. Or at least try and remember as much as you can of what you forgot.

Steve Allen acquires 2,000-Year-Old-Man's Secrets of Longevity.

1. Don't run for a bus—there'll always be another.

2. Never, ever touch fried food.

3. Stay out of a Ferrari or any other small Italian car.

4. Eat fruit—a nectarine—even a rotten plum is good.

Source: *Mel Brooks, as quoted in Jon Winokur, Friendly Advice, copyright 1990 by Jon Winokur.*

This old gent from Hooverville, *Ohio made it to old age, but isn't all sure it was worth it. According to him, "No man in the United States has had the trouble I had since 1931. No man. Don't talk to me. I'm deaf. I lost my farm in 1931. I went into town to work as a painter. I fell off a scaffold and broke my leg. I went to work in an acid factory. I got acid spilt on me; burnt my nose and made me blind. Then I get these awful headaches. I've been to lots of doctors, but that doesn't help me."*

When you get to age 50, you can expect to:

...live at least 31.5 more years, provided you're a female. That's a life expectancy increase of seven years over ladies who turned 50 in 1944. If you're a male, the average number of years left for you is 26.7, an increase of five years. Take care of yourself, or she gets it all!

...grow old more healthily than your predecessors. Recent studies indicate that , though science has not figured out how we can live forever, we should expect to live well into a healthy old age and then die suddenly, without the long decline many of our parents suffered through.

...live a very full life with an artificial organ, if one is required. Today, such implants as artificial joints, cardiac pacemakers and lens implants for the eye are virtually permanent aids or replacements for defective or lost body parts that enable their users to live almost normal lives. In the next few years, most of today's implants will have been succeeded by far better models, and there is a good chance that doctors will at least be able to replace the human heart with an artificial one by the turn of the century, or soon after.

...be able to handle personal computers as easily as the kids. In a very short time, these high tech systems will be versatile, multimedia, interactive powerhouses and will comprehend your commands quickly and easily. You talk, and your computer will log appointments, book reservations, look up addresses, calculate travel time, copy, print—practically everything but lick the stamp (which probably won't be necessary).

...miss the AIDS plague. In the 1990s, AIDS will kill at least 25 times as many Americans as died in the Vietnam war. Aren't you glad your roaming years are behind you? Other good news is that, by the year 2000, the great plague of the twentieth century should be over. So wait until then to have your late-life sexual crisis.

...live in a mobile home, if you so desire, without feeling like a social outcast. Remember when mobile homes were considered eyesores? Well, times have changed. Since World War II, mobile homes have become affordable (average price $27,800), livable, comfortable, and, most importantly, acceptable. In the last 50 years, mobile homes have increased 25 times in number. No other type of housing has grown so dramatically.

...qualify as a member of the largest association in the country, the American Association of Retired Persons. One of the benefits is that you'll now be able to join 22,879,886 other folks and receive *Modern Maturity.* Welcome aboard! Have a great life! Live to be 125!

50 things you can buy today that weren't available in the forties.

1. A CD player
2. Running shoes
3. Mini van
4. A Slinky
5. A hula hoop
6. A football tee
7. An all-titanium driver
8. A calculator
9. A giant screen TV set
10. A color TV set
11. A cordless phone
12. Filter cigarettes
13. Handi Wipes
14. Saran Wrap
15. A VCR
16. Nylon stockings
17. Lean Cuisine
18. A ball point pen
19. Chocolate chip cookies
20. Ping irons
21. Bulls tickets
22. A personal computer
23. A barbecue grill
24. A one man chain saw
25. Vanity plates
26. An electric carving knife
27. A pager
28. Bubble gum
29. A Mickey Mantle baseball card
30. Pop Tarts
31. Vodka
32. Non stop tickets to L.A.
33. Bagels outside New York
34. Miller Lite
35. Polyester suits
36. A laser disc player
37. A self propelled lawn mower
38. A blood pressure monitor
39. A treadmill
40. A camcorder
41. A steam iron
42. An espresso maker
43. A portable food mixer
44. An electric toothbrush
45. Starbucks Coffee
46. A leaf shredder
47. A paint stripper
48. Frozen yogurt
49. Paper towels
50. Roller blades

Where in the world are you going to live the rest of your life?

Lots of people your (our) age have always dreamed of sailing off to distant places. But few really plan to live on a boat the rest of their lives.

Many consider the Sun Belt states, while others plan on staying right where they are. Still others actually move, not just to different states, but to different countries. Hey, when you don't have a timeclock to punch, anything's possible.

And if you want to live a long, full life, there is good reason to not only get out of town, but out of the country. Which country? We ask you to consider these facts:

In Istanbul, Xaro Agha had a great life. He fathered a child at age 90, and lived to be 164.

In England, Thomas Parr lived through the reigns of 10 English monarchs and died at age 152.

In the U.S.S.R, Mahmud Eivazov had three sons who lived past 100 and a daughter who made it to 123. Mahmud himself was born in 1803 and celebrated his 150th birthday in 1958.

In Jerusalem, Mohammed Khalil Abdul Hawa celebrated his 136th birthday in 1957.

In Ecuador, Gabriel Erazo lived in the Valley of Vilcabamba, and was still doing a full day's work in his garden in 1973, at age 130. According to Gabriel, that wasn't that unusual. An amazing 1% of his neighbors were centenarians.

In Canada, Caesar Paul was an Algonquin Indian who died in Pembroke, Ontario, at age 112.

And none of the people from any of these countries lived in the countries most noted for longevity. If you're a woman and wish to live a really long life, consider the countries on the list below.

The 10 Countries where the highest percent of women live to be 85 years old:

1.	Puerto Rico	33.7%
2.	Canada	33.6
3.	Sweden	33.3
4.	Netherlands	32.0
5.	Norway	31.8
6.	France	31.6
7.	U.S.	30.8
8.	Denmark	30.5
9.	Bermuda	30.4
10.	Hong Kong	30.3

Source: *United Nations Demographic Yearbook 1993*

So what are you going to do after you turn 90?

Amos Alonzo Stagg continued coaching football. In his mid eighties, in 1943, he was named NCAA coach of the year for his job at College of Pacific. In his nineties, he was a specialist coach at Stockton Junior College in California. He retired from coaching at around 98.

Armand Hammer was the head of Occidental Petroleum. He was 91.

Hulda Crooks climbed Mt. Whitney. She was 91.

Paul Spangler ran a marathon and set a world swimming record (for folks over 90). He swam 1,500 meters in 52 minutes, 41.53 seconds. He was 92.

Dame Judith Anderson, actress, gave a one hour benefit performance. She was 93.

George Burns performed at Proctor's Theater in Schenectady, New York—63 years after his first performance there. He was 94.

Martha Graham choreographed a dance performance. She was 95.

Kathrine Robinson Everett was practicing law in North Carolina. At age 96.

Martin Miller was working full-time lobbying for senior citizens in Indiana. At age 97.

Beatrice Wood, ceramist, exhibited her last work at age 98.

Kin Natrita and Gin Kanie, twin sisters, recorded a hit CD single in Japan and starred in a television commercial. They were 99.

Mieczyslaw Horszowski, the classical pianist, recorded a new album at age 99.

David Ray, of Franklin, Tennessee, decided it was time to learn to read. He was 99.

If you were born in the country...

...you remember way back when, back when folks let time pass at its own pace, with grace and dignity and, even laziness; back when the little things in a day had a lot more significance.

In those days that have surely gone by, a person could spend half a morning at the store doing nothing very important without feeling one pang of guilt.

We called it the country store. And that didn't bother us a whit. Country was a good thing to be back then.

It might have taken you a good hour to investigate the latest needlepoint fly swatters the widow lady down the lane had brought in. Shoot, you could lose another 15 minutes just testing the homemade brooms sticking out of one of the barrels next to the weighing apparatus provided by the Detroit Automatic Scale Co.

For some reason, the cold sodas tasted colder then. And the candy didn't come in wrappers. Even the licorice was out, standing up proud and colorful in the big clear jars next to the gumdrops and sour balls. And whatever happened to rock candy?

If you needed a nail, that could take you another 15 minutes. They displayed the big ones in those wooden bins along the wall, clearly marked and fairly priced: a whole penny for 10 of the big ones.

In the winter, you could sit in a rocker next to the potbellied stove as long as you wanted, provided you bought some cracker barrel biscuits or maybe a slab of cheese on your way out. Come the first warm day of spring, passing up a game of checkers with the old timers on the front porch was real difficult.

You could even get your blood pressure checked at the country store–providing the doc wasn't off tending to somebody's colicky mule. And when you went across the street to get the mail, didn't the postmaster always know your name on a P.O.-box-number basis and always have time to ask about the family?

Funny isn't it, that we never had to rush home to see the soaps. There weren't any, of course, but Jack Benny didn't come on the radio 'til nightfall. And even though we had to go home and cook dinner, seems like we had more time than we do now, even when we're serving TV dinners.

Back then, people like Zimmerman and Hapgood owned stores; they weren't just names stuck in telephone books.

All jams were homemade, fruit was never frozen and you had to crank the telephone but that was all right because you didn't use it 'cept for emergencies.

There was no Ace Hardware store. But even though a fellow like Orville Jackson sold everything from cradles to caskets and watches, horseshoes, health needs and did veterinary on the side, he never was known to run out of anything.

Well, thanks for taking the time to read this. If nothing else, it shows you're not in a hurry. Have a real happy day, hear?

245

If you were born in the city...

...probably the main thing you remember is how busy everybody was. Mothers were cooking overtime, trying to make tasty dinners out of things that just weren't meant to go together, like carrots and oranges and cornbread, and she was forever complaining that the ration box never had enough stamps in it.

Everybody was into saving. The boys got the job of stacking and turning in the tin cans and newspaper stacks, and little sisters got the job of winding string and wadding up tin foil onto the big ball. And everybody saved bacon grease in an old coffee can. Big sis, of course, had this big bag of nylons to turn in, but by the time those socks hit that bag there was darned little nylon left. Sis was also the one who bought that eyebrow pencil back in '43 and would try to draw a straight line down the back of her leg to make it look like a seam...and it always came out crooked.

Looking good was a big deal. You didn't want holes in your clothes like they do today. Since new things were so hard to come by, wearing old wasn't near the thing it is today. Nobody would ever think of washing a new pair of pants prior to wearing 'em.

It was also important to be like everybody else. We didn't yet know the real meaning of individuality. Fads caught on fast, but we just assumed that everybody started them. If a group of kids over in New York started wearing striped socks, before you knew it everybody in the country was wearing striped stocks–until whoever it was who started that trend switched to something else like wide cuffs or, remember this: no cuffs at all? To keep up with this one, there for a while, we would pin the bottoms of our pants up inside so they wouldn't be ruined when you had to change to some other fashion statement.

Oh, you had to be very resourceful to keep up with the times of 1944. The city person's version of the country store was the corner store and, yes, it usually was on a corner, though it didn't have to be. What it really was was the hangout, the most important place in your life. This is where you stayed in touch. And, it was the only place in the world where you could get a cherry coke. You see, the coke was mixed, live, and the cherry flavoring was added to it. You couldn't do that at home, nor would you want to. Some tweepy couples of the day would share milk shakes, one glass–two straws, but if you were real cool, you didn't do that.

Wheels weren't yet important. Nobody had them, and if you did, you couldn't get gas. So we just didn't think about cars.

Movies were big, especially Saturday matinees. We were very religious about this, and Hollywood knew it. They use to run serials for us–to be continued next Saturday, same time, same place.

And we all loved radio. On Sunday nights, everybody came inside, even on hot summer evenings, to listen to Jack Benny and then George and Gracie. And when Joe Louis or Sugar Ray or Rocky Graziano fought, (Rocky usually fought Tony Zale), the streets were really empty. And we all stayed in daily touch with where the boys were overseas, and who was winning which battle. Everybody had somebody close at the front, and it was significant when we got one of those flimsy white letters with red and blue markings. That was always a great day.

If these contemporaries had lived as long as you, here's how old they'd be in 1997:

John F. Kennedy would be 80.

Jack Kerouac would be 75.

Judy Garland would be 75.

Rocky Marciano would be 74.

Malcom X would be 72.

Robert F. Kennedy would be 72.

Marilyn Monroe would be 71.

Martin Luther King, Jr. would be 68.

Anne Frank would be 68.

James Dean would be 66.

Elvis Presley would be 62.

John Lennon would be 57.

Otis Redding would be 56.

Jimi Hendrix would be 55.

Janis Joplin would be 54.

John Belushi would be 48.

THE SHAPE